RECORDS OF ACHIEVEMENT

Kogan Page Books for Teachers series
Series Editor: Tom Marjoram

RECORDS OF ACHIEVEMENT

ISSUES AND PRACTICE

Geoffrey Hall

Books for Teachers
Series Editor: Tom Marjoram

KOGAN
PAGE

First published in 1989 by Kogan Page Ltd
120 Pentonville Road, London N1 9JN

Typeset by DP Photosetting, Aylesbury, Bucks
Printed and bound in Great Britain by
Biddles Ltd, Guildford

British Library Cataloguing in Publication Data

Hall, Geoffrey
    Records of achievement: Issues and
    practice
    1. Schools. Students. Academic achievement
    Assessment. Marking & reporting
    I. Title
    371.2'72

    ISBN 1-85091-674-8

Contents

6
Records of Achievement and the National Curriculum 109

Acknowledgements

During the research for this book it was heartening to meet so many dedicated and committed teachers, not least those working at Brant High School. To them I would like to express my sincere thanks for their cooperation in allowing me to observe meetings, arranging interviews and giving access to unpublished materials. Without the willing assistance of Brant's records of achievement coordinators and the senior management team, this manuscript could not have been written. Their identification with the philosophy underpinning records of achievement has much to commend to others contemplating entering this field.

I must also thank Winton LEA for supporting my monitoring of the pilot scheme, Mrs Eileen Shaw the NPRA Development Officer for her generous help with survey material and Ray Derricott of Liverpool University Department of Education whose invaluable support and inspiration convinced me I could complete the task. He also read the text and made helpful comments on the draft, as did Dolores Black and Tom Marjoram of Kogan Page. Finally, thanks are due in no small degree to my family for the sacrifices they made in supporting my endeavours.

I am also indebted to the following for permission to reproduce material:

The NPRA for the record of achievement validation statements and extracts from a document on accreditation.

Her Majesty's Stationery Office for Paragraph 11 of *Records of Achievement: A Statement of Policy*, and Figure 1 of the *National Curriculum Task Group on Assessment and Testing Report – A digest for schools*.

Winton LEA for Figure 2 the Unit Pro-forma.

Frodsham High School for the extract from their coordinated science guide.

Secondary Examination Council for Appendix 1, the Appendices A and B of the SEC Draft Criteria Geography Report.

Jeff Brewer of Hookergate School for the cartoon.

St Edmund Arrowsmith RC School (Figure 4).

St Peters RC School, Wigan (Figure 6).

... AND SO AS I BRING THIS BRIEF INTRODUCTION TO THE PROBLEMS OF PROFILING TO A CLOSE MAY I JUST ADD ...
4TH YEAR PROFILING GROUP.
JEFF BREWER

Introduction

Unlike much of the literature devoted to profiles and records of achievement, this book focuses on the issues arising from the experience of one school in the Northern Partnership for Records of Achievement (NPRA) Pilot Study. This approach has been chosen because it is felt that the problems encountered are likely to be or have been met in one form or other in schools nationally as they grapple with the implications of the DES Statement of Policy (1984), such projects as the Technical and Vocational Education Initiative (TVEI) and, more daunting still, the prospect of the national curriculum. In order that this perspective does not have a parochial flavour it is broadened, where appropriate, by cross-referencing these concerns with the practice of other institutions in the NPRA Pilot Study and the research findings of the DES Pilot Schemes.

However, probably an equally compelling reason for choosing this course is that the school in question has received only a modest increase in resources to cope with an innovation which is far reaching in the changes which have to be adopted. It is felt that an analysis of this kind of situation is likely to have more credibility than that where records of achievement are being promoted with the assistance of national funding. The emphasis is on the 11–16 age range because this is where the main thrust of Government policy lies. It is not the purpose of this book to appraise the profiling initiatives of such organisations as the City and Guilds of London Institute (CGLI), Royal Society of Arts (RSA), Youth Training Scheme (YTS) and others. However, many of the issues discussed here have relevance in the context of these schemes.

After a short introductory history outlining the massive growth in interest in the subject, Chapter 1 examines three dimensions in the development. First, the contribution of the examination system is analysed in terms of the attempts to move from the limited information given by GCE/CSE grades to the more informative profiling of results which would be the outcome of the grade-related criteria (GRC) exercise, which was undertaken in the mid-1980s. Second, the importance of the students' role is analysed and how it is seen by the protagonists as being central to recording achievement. Political recognition of the significance of these trends is also outlined culminating with the DES Statement of Policy in 1984. Accountability, the third dimension, underpins the other two; first, in terms of the needs of students, and second, with regard to parents and the wider community of users. An element of it is the assurance they will require concerning the validity of records, and the implications of this in terms of accreditation are touched upon.

Chapter 2 first explains the background to the formation of the NPRA then looks at the merits of its unit accreditation schemes which are in some ways unique. Each unit is a record of achievement in itself. The schemes' main virtue is that it can give credit in the form of statements of achievement and later letters of credit to students of all abilities within a short time of them achieving the unit outcomes, thus promoting increased student motivation. The remainder of the chapter outlines the background of Brant High School and analyses the context into which the NPRA Pilot Study for records of achievement was introduced.

An area, often given little attention in the literature – subject recording – is considered in Chapter 3. First, the pros and cons of adopting such a model are examined in relation to the alternative cross-curricular approach, and the question of time and resources is discussed. This is followed by an exploration of the problems which departments have encountered in setting up recording systems. These range from the identification of criteria and computerised comment banks to the recording of personal attributes and the participation of students.

In Chapter 4 the focus shifts to reviewing in the context of the tutor/student relationship. The benefits are outlined from the standpoint of school, tutor and student, and the question of disadvantage raised. The claim that records of achievement increase student motivation is examined, as is the place of the summative document in this context. The organisation of reviewing is considered in terms of alternatives to the one-to-one relationship, time and frequency implications, planned and impromptu discussions, the value of log books and student access. There is no doubt that the group tutor role takes on a new significance with the introduction of records of achievement.

Chapter 5 sees the culmination of Brant's efforts in the form of the summative record of achievement. Two examples are included as reference points for discussion (one in the text, the other in the

Appendices). The problem of brevity in relation to student ownership and users' needs is discussed in connection with the view of employers' associations. This theme is continued in relation to what can be included in the testimonial, and the problems of verification and context are considered. The latter emerges as a concern of the subject departments as does the place of information technology. The role of students is then looked at in terms of their contribution to the summative document and how they might use it. With regard to employers' views on its composition, the issues of negative comments, objectivity, consistency and standardisation are explored. The place of records of achievement with reference to parents' needs follows and is considered at length.

The latter half of this chapter is concerned with the role of management and accreditation. Concerning the former, which is quite fundamental to the development of records of achievement, this is viewed with reference to the commitment and leadership of senior management, corporate development and the coordination role. The contribution LEAs might make is also spelt out. Finally, accreditation is discussed as a necessary part of the accountability process and particular regional proposals are examined, drawing on experience from Canada.

Chapter 6 looks to the future with the advent of the national curriculum. The place of records of achievement in this context is reviewed in relation to the seven principles which the Government has adopted in response to the proposals of the Task Group on Assessment and Testing (TGAT). In this connection, such issues as standardisation and teacher ownership, student participation, the specification of profile components and achievement levels, and the place of cross-curricular skills are considered; together with parental involvement, the relationship between GCSE and achievement levels, and socio-economic factors which might influence achievement. The impact of TGAT on curriculum review is also discussed. Lastly, the question is asked, Where do records of achievement stand in this unique situation?

Chapter 1

Records of Achievement, Why?
– Rationale and Response

It seems almost an impertinence to raise this question when teachers have been recording pupils' achievement throughout the history of education. It has been seen as the obvious acknowledgement of success whether it has been a tick, comment, grade, mark or other form of reward. Why is it then that a records of achievement 'industry' has grown up, culminating with the Secretaries of State for England and Wales sanctioning a major project of ten pilot schemes with funding of £2 million per year for three to five years?[1]

Some important developments

This explosion of interest has occurred in a period of less than a decade. In 1980 the Schools Council commissioned a survey of developments in this area, and Janet Balogh, who presented the results, found that only 25 schools in the country were operating profiles.[2] However, the statistic may be misleading because some of the schools surveyed could have been using systems of recording which they did not call a profile or record of achievement. This reservation apart, the rate of growth can be appreciated by the fact that, in 1987, the National Profiling Network[3] reported on 104 schemes to its 300 member schools.

However, the Council's role in promoting a wider and more diagnostic approach to identifying achievement has not been confined to the Balogh survey. The Progress in Learning Science Project asked the question 'what do we need to know about children to help their learning?' and involved groups of teachers in devising checklists to provide a framework for observing such behaviours.[4] This was one of the earlier attempts at 'comment banks' based on agreed objectives and covering the age range from five to thirteen years. This kind of development was endorsed in its Working Paper 70, *The Practical Curriculum*,[5] and received 'pump priming' funding from its Programme 2. With regard to the latter, the Council assisted a small group of secondary schools in the Metropolitan Borough of Knowsley who were developing a more diagnostic approach to reporting subject specific skills performance.[6]

Alongside these trends, a group of Her Majesty's Inspectors (HMI) were also attempting to identify subject skill areas, how such skills might be assessed and where there was overlap. This development emerged from the idea of 'an entitlement curriculum' which was the concern of a Department of Education and Science (DES) Short Course at Oxford in 1976; later to be strongly endorsed by Mr James Callaghan's speech at Ruskin College also in that year. A legacy of this and the Cheshire work referred to below, has been the chapter devoted to assessment in *History in the Primary and Secondary Years - An HMI View* published in 1985. This draws upon the framework of objectives put forward by Coltham and Fines (1971),[7] but also has taken into account the criticisms of Gard and Lee[8] regarding this essentially 'behavioural' objectives approach to the subject. Thus, *History in the Primary and Secondary Years* has presented teachers with a framework for assessment based upon the criteria of reference and information-finding skills, skills in chronology, language and historical ideas, empathetic understanding, asking historical questions, and synthesis and communication at five levels of performance.

During this period initiatives were also being taken in schools. An unpublished HMI survey of history in Cheshire schools noted that during the period 1976–1983 there had been a marked shift towards a range of skill assessments. The mark book had become redundant! In 1980 Mr Gerry Wilson, then Head of History at Parkway School, Knowsley, produced a departmental policy statement exemplifying this approach. This led to the department assessing the subject on the basis of evidence, empathy development, conceptual understanding, synthesis, reference and information skills. Both these developments and others in Knowsley owe much to the influence of Brian Chaplin HMI whose contribution to a DES Short Course at Liverpool University in 1979 pointed the way towards a broader, more diagnostic view of recording achievement.

Definitions

It is important at this point to define the terms 'profile' and 'record of achievement' because they are often used as if they are one and the same. Hitchcock[9] defines a profile as

... a document which can record assessments of students across a wide range of abilities, including skills, attitudes, personal achievements; it frequently involves the student in its formation, and has a formative as well as a summative function.

Formative refers to the collection of data which, as the National Profiling Network[10] puts it '... serves to fashion the way or direction in which a student develops'. It goes on to define *formative recording* as 'a process involving some discussion between teacher and pupil affecting both the course to be followed and the pupil's progress'. It will be noted that the authors see the student as a participant in this exercise. Indeed, this may appear to be stating the obvious and the essential, but, as will be seen later in discussing implementation, the involvement of students in their assessment is one of the more difficult aspects of recording achievement.

A record of achievement, on the other hand, may include profiles of a variety of skills, attitudes, personal achievements, etc, and results in public examinations. It is widely called a summative record, or leaving document, in which the formative record is summarised for the benefit of a user who does not know the student. This summarising exercise is, in effect, taking place throughout a student's school life as decisions have to be made on what is to be reported to parents and upon what evidence choice of options, examination courses, etc is made. For the purpose of this book 'profile' and 'record of achievement' may be used interchangeably because the literature reflects this use of the terms.

The contribution of the examination system

It can be argued that one of the reasons for the growth of profiles/records was the dissatisfaction with examination results as a means of recording performance. In the Appendices to the Beloe Report, *Secondary School Examinations other than GCE* published in 1960, extracts from the Spens (1938), Norwood (1943), and Crowther (1959) Reports all point to the limitations of examination results in describing performance, and make the plea for the development of school records or leaving certificates which might give a broader view of students' achievements. *Half Our Future* (the Newsom Report) in 1963 asserted that 'Boys and girls who stay at school until they are 16 may reasonably look for some record of achievement when they leave.'

This point is reinforced by the Schools Council's enquiry into the attitudes of early school leavers, *Enquiry I: Young School Leavers* (1968) and admirably summarised by the Schools Council's *Working Paper*

53, The Whole Curriculum 13–16 (1975).[11] It stated,

> We believe that all pupils should be offered a documentary record at the completion of their secondary schooling. This record should be a balanced account of the pupil's attainments, interests and aspirations. This document should be externally validated and underwritten by appropriately authorised bodies.

This assertion not only supports the demand for a wider view to be taken of recording achievement, but implies that such a record might be accredited in some way. This vision has become DES policy[12] and will be discussed in greater detail in later chapters.

Identifying achievement by profiling grade-related criteria

At the centre of the debate is the limitation of the General Certificate of Education (GCE)/Certificate of Secondary Education (CSE) examination grades in describing performance. They are norm referenced and tell us little more than where pupils stand in relation to their peers. They are global rather than diagnostic in nature. It has been argued that this mitigates strongly against lower-attaining pupils. For example, it has been said that employers will have little regard for Grade F or G performances in the General Certificate of Secondary Education (GCSE) examination, despite F being considered the national average. It has been suggested that if students' performance against the criteria used for the awarding of grades was made explicit, this would be more helpful to the students and employers alike.

This idea received strong support from Sir Keith Joseph, then Secretary of State for Education and Science. In 1984, in his speech to the North of England Education Conference, he said, 'We need a reasonable assurance that pupils obtaining a particular grade will know certain things and possess certain skills or have achieved a certain competence.' In response to this the Secondary Examinations Council (SEC) set up in July 1984 11 subject working parties to develop grade criteria in biology, chemistry, craft, design and technology (CDT), English, French, geography, history, mathematics, physics, science and Welsh first language. Later, a further 13 began work, and by September 1987 the first 10, plus German, social science, art and design, classical subjects, music and religious studies had reported. As a result of these reports the SEC recommended that a profile report be employed on the examination certificate.[13]

Clearly, if this could be implemented, and certification included descriptions of positive achievements in relation to grades, students of all abilities would benefit in that their strengths would be identified, and yet, at the same time, their performance would be graded in relation to their peers. However, translating the draft grade criteria into the examination of particular syllabuses has not been an easy task. To understand the nature of the problems encountered, it is important to be aware of the exercise undertaken by the working parties.

The subject working parties commenced their work in the knowledge that previous research[14] into the possibility of criterion referencing in examinations such as GCE and CSE had suggested that it would be unlikely that they would be able to produce grade criteria that would be sufficiently explicit as to the knowledge and skill achieved by a candidate at a particular grade in the subject *as a whole*. As the report of the Working Party for Geography Draft Grade Related Criteria (GRC)[15] puts it,

> In our system of examining we allow candidates to offset weaknesses in some areas of a subject against strengths in others. Because of this trade-off between aspects of a subject, candidates who obtain a particular grade may show very few things in common across the subject as a whole, and attempts to describe in general terms what candidates achieving a particular grade in a subject can do, have resulted in extremely vague statements. The grade descriptions in the National Criteria for GCSE exemplify this problem.

With this in mind, the SEC invited the working parties to divide their subjects into domains and establish criteria for the award of Grades F, C and A across the domains. A domain was defined 'as a collection of the elements of a subject that forms some reasonably coherent subset of skills and competencies needed in the subject'.[16]

This task was far from easy and the difficulties encountered by the working parties were also met at the next stage which was to conduct trials. Teams of examiners attempted to apply the draft grade criteria by re-marking the work produced by candidates in their 1986 examinations. 'This has been compared to trying on an ill-fitting suit – it touches in some places but that doesn't mean it fits.'[17]

A fundamental area of concern was the view taken of the subject, not only by teachers, but also to be found in the national criteria. For example, geography and English are seen as unitary subjects whereas the grade criteria exercise separates them into domains. It will be seen later that school subject departments, in developing a more diagnostic approach to recording achievement, have also found this to be a contentious area. The examiners' task was first to separate the examination questions into the domains and then mark them using the GRC. Rogers,[18] describing the experience of the University of London School Examinations Board (ULSEB) which looked at six subjects – biology, physics, chemistry, geography, history and CDT – found

> None of the examination papers fitted comfortably into the draft grade criteria and it was often impossible to separate examination questions into the different domains. For example, what, ask the exasperated researchers, is the difference between having 'specific geographical knowledge' and 'geographical understanding'? In history, the SEC expects examination boards to distinguish between 'interpret' and 'reach a judgement'.

Rogers goes on to argue,

> It [ULSEB] also found imbalances in the way marks would have to be allocated. SEC criteria insist on equal marks for each domain. [Rogers is referring here to the equal weighting given to each.] But this proved impossible, especially with subjects offering a range of paper or subject options.

It is important to note here that, as the SEC[19] has pointed out, the exercise was with 'the practicability of using *subject based grade criteria* as a basis for marking examinations which are necessarily *syllabus based*' [my italics]. Furthermore, despite these criticisms the SEC considered the exercise a success overall. In its press notice of September 1987 it stated,

> There were inevitable differences of view among the examiners as to whether draft grade criteria were more or less readily applicable to examinations on their syllabuses or indeed whether as subject experts they would have necessarily produced similar criteria for teaching purposes, *but in general they agreed on the value of the testing of marking schemes prepared in the style of, and at the detailed level of the draft criteria, and that this should be done as soon as possible in the GCSE context*' [my italics].

In light of this experience the SEC is pressing ahead with a pilot scheme commencing in 1988 for examination in 1990. Each of the examination groups involved has selected a GCSE syllabus in mathematics, and also one which meets the new draft National Criteria for the Sciences: Double Award. For each syllabus the groups' examiners will be asked what positive qualities or attributes the course is intended to develop in the candidate, which they will be looking for in awarding marks and grades in the examinations on the syllabus. This list will form one axis of what will be called a 'performance matrix'. The other axis is to be used to indicate the different levels of achievement to be expected in relation to each attribute from candidates who have followed the course and taken the examination.

Two points arise from these developments. Even if the pilot scheme is successful, it is not known whether the experience is fully or partially transferable to other subject syllabuses, and, secondly, whether the resulting 'profile' will be acceptable. To appreciate how such a profile might read, the Appendices A and B from the Draft Criteria Geography Report (see Appendix 1) suggests that the profile report would be substantial. It will be seen that five domains have been proposed, level one refers to GCSE grade F; level three, grade C; and level four, grade A. The working party had also been asked to define a further level of achievement by grade criteria at around the mid-point of grade E and this was seen as being an extension of level one. In this instance only a preliminary statement was made. The students' final grade would be arrived at by an aggregation of the domain scores employing 'hurdles' where any domains or domain scores were to be considered a prerequisite.[20]

The above discussion has centred around developments aimed at making the description of the summative examination performance more informative. But it is worth noting that the course work element of the GCSE (worth at least 20 per cent of the marks in most subjects) is a profiling exercise. In the case of the Sciences: Double Award, the whole examination is based on the recording of performance against a variety of criteria over a three-year period commencing at the beginning of year three.[21] An extract from the record of achievement completed by the student and teacher at Frodsham High School, Cheshire, can be found in Appendix 2.

These developments suggest a movement away from a system of recording performance, dominated by the limited amount of information given by a grade, to a more diagnostic approach. However, while progress has been made in formative recording, the time when all GCSE results are characterized by a profile appears to be some way off.

The student dimension

The above discussion has been concerned with how our national system of examining can be developed to give more information about students' performance. Even if this development is successful it would only partially answer the case for a broad picture of students' skills, competencies and achievements. Furthermore, the wider issue of involving students in their own learning, of which assessment and recording is a central part, has still to be addressed.

The broader view of performance and achievement and the students' role in it have become the focal points of the record of achievement debate. To appreciate what is involved, it is useful to follow the developments which have led to the present position.

First, involving students in the learning process in partnership with their teachers, as opposed to being passive recipients of knowledge, has a history which Black and Broadfoot[22] trace back to Charlotte Mason's work in the 1860s and the Dalton Plan in the USA. Much of good practice in primary schools with respect to the integrated day and individualised learning assignments had its roots in this early work. Indeed, a stereotype began to emerge in the 1950s of the primary schools being 'child-centred', while secondary schools were 'subject-centred'. The latter label was acquired because many people considered that the examination system, being largely subject-based, exercised too much control over the curriculum of the secondary school. This dominance, however, Burgess and Adams[23] argue, has lessened as some teachers have taken steps to become actively involved in assessment procedures, initially through CSE Mode 3 and, more recently, through teacher-controlled examining at 16+. Of course, as indicated earlier, even larger numbers are now participating with the advent of GCSE.

Burgess and Adams go on to suggest that some teachers are moving towards a third level at which 'students are positively involved with their teachers in planning, recording and assessing their individual purposes, programmes and progress'. An example of this style of teaching in action would be the City and Guilds 365 Vocational Preparation course. The essence of this process is that learning takes place through the medium of a partnership between teacher and student. It can be argued that this has always been the case. The difference here is that the student's contribution is considerable. How equal the partnership is will depend upon the nature of the teacher--pupil relationship, the interpersonal skills of the teacher and the ethos of the institution concerned.

The outcomes of this relationship are claimed to be:

- It increases student motivation and self-awareness.
- Students feel more valued if they are significantly involved in the learning process. This, in turn, is reflected in a positive attitude towards the aims of the institution.
- It enables the diagnosis of students' strengths and weaknesses to

take place so that individual learning targets can be set.
- The process informs teaching and guidance in that objectives, content and style can be modified.
- It follows from the previous point that inservice training needs will be revealed which can provide the basis for staff development programmes.
- If students are involved in the compilation of a summative or interim summative document, they are likely to value it more.

Acceptance of the students' role

These claims have largely been accepted by a wide range of bodies. In 1972 the Headmasters' Association of Scotland established a working party in conjunction with the Scottish Council for Research in Education (SCRE) to develop and evaluate a new assessment and reporting procedure. The Association was concerned particularly about the current examination system forcing pupils into two unrealistic categories – certificate and non-certificate; and also about the non-certificate pupils who would leave school at 16 without a national certificate. In its aims it called for:

> ... a comprehensive picture of their [the students'] attitudes and interests so as to enable responsible guidance staff to give them the best possible advice on future curricular and/or vocational choice, and on appropriate social and leisure activities ...

This may appear a one-way communication but the value of a wide view of achievement is recognised. And, to give credit where it is due, in its report, *Pupils in Profile*,[24] considerable importance is attached to teacher/pupil consultation. This is seen as the role of the guidance teacher. In England and Wales this responsibility would probably fall upon the shoulders of the form tutor. The interesting point here is that student consultation is not seen as a role for the subject specialist. This raises the question regarding the contribution they can be expected to make to records of achievement. This issue is discussed later.

In England and Wales the response has also been positive. In 1983 the National Union of Teachers, in its publication *Pupil Profiles*, supported the introduction of profiles, calling them valuable diagnostic instruments:

> ... which can lead to appropriate changes in teaching and learning strategies, and which involves the pupil in the assessment process, thus enhancing motivation and understanding.

In her survey of over 100 teachers and lecturers in Avon (1983), Hitchcock found staff generally supportive of the idea. She writes,

> Among the most striking findings were that virtually all teachers who had been involved with profiling believed they were helping their students, that student motivation was increased, and that any extra work was therefore worthwhile.[25]

In the Further Education Unit (FEU) publication *Profiles in Action*, profiles produced by such agencies as the Royal Society of Arts (RSA), the Business and Technician Education Council (B/Tec), the City and Guilds Institute (CGLI) and the Youth Training Programme (YTP), all aspire to provide the benefits identified above. It is interesting at this point to note that these bodies, operating mainly in post-16 education, were first in the field to offer 'national profiles'. Bearing in mind the student-centred focus of the work it might have been expected that such developments would have originated in the primary sector.

It is probably fair to say that such profiles filled a void in the tertiary sector. However, as there was (and still is) a clientele with common aspirations in secondary education, served by such developments as the Technical and Vocational and Education Initiative (TVEI) and the Low Attaining Pupils Project (LAPP), and a large number of schools who felt there was an urgent need for reform of the 14–16 curriculum for low-attaining pupils, many 11–16 institutions introduced RSA, B/Tec or CGLI courses. The growing use of these profiles is acknowledged in Para 3 of the DES Policy Statement[26] and may, unintentionally, have created pressure for a national policy to be established.

Political recognition

At the party political level, all the major parties supported the introduction of records of achievement at the 1987 General Election. Labour, in its publication *Labour's Charter for Pupils and Parents* (1985) stated,

> We want all pupils at the age of 16 to be awarded a profile of achievement. This would include the results of public examinations for all pupils, the continuous assessment of the progress made in sections of courses completed throughout secondary schooling, and pupils' overall contribution to the life of the school. We see these different methods of assessment complementing one another; but in the longer term, we expect the continuous element of the profile of achievement to be seen of greater value as 'educational currency' than the more traditional examinations.

23

Purposes of records of achievement

The Secretaries of State believe that there are four main purposes which records of achievement and the associated recording systems should serve. These purposes overlap to some extent.

i. Recognition of achievement. Records and recording systems should recognise, acknowledge and give credit for what pupils have achieved and experienced, not just in terms of results in public examinations but in other ways as well. They should do justice to pupils' own efforts and to the efforts of teachers, parents, ratepayers and taxpayers to give them a good education.

ii. Motivation and personal development. They should contribute to pupils' personal development and progress by improving their motivation, providing encouragement and increasing their awareness of strengths, weaknesses and opportunities.

iii. Curriculum and organisation. The recording process should help schools to identify the all round potential of their pupils and to consider how well their curriculum, teaching and organisation enable pupils to develop the general, practical and social skills which are to be recorded.

iv. A document of record. Young people leaving school or college should take with them a short, summary document of record which is recognised and valued by employers and institutions of further and higher education. This should provide a more rounded picture of candidates for jobs or courses than can be provided by a list of examination results, thus helping potential users to decide how candidates could best be employed, or for which jobs, training schemes or courses they are likely to be suitable.

Figure 1 *Extract from* Records of Achievement: A Statement of Policy, *Department of Education and Science Welsh Office*

With the Alliance parties accepting the idea, the DES committed through the purposes in its policy statement (see Figure 1), and the remarkable growth in schools and Local Education Authorities (LEAs) identified at the beginning of this chapter, the lay person could be forgiven for thinking that the case for records of achievement had been fully accepted and implemented. In practice, the all-embracing nature of the innovation, which follows from the decision to record in the broadest possible way students' achievements, puts considerable pressure on institutions, and it is not surprising that there is resistance and misunderstanding.

Accountability

Before closing this chapter it is necessary to discuss the accountability dimension of records of achievement. Goacher,[27] writing in 1983, argued that the development of records during the previous four years had been in response to a number of shortcomings in the education system, one of which was

> ... a need for greater accountability on the part of schools and teachers in their reporting to parents, to employers, to their students and to each other; attempts which lead to more detailed reporting and more analytical methods of presenting information.

The emphasis here is on 'greater', and this has been a feature of educational development during the last decade. It is not unfair to say that the response from schools was patchy, but early leaders in this field such as the Sutton Centre, Comberton College and Evesham High School, were strongly motivated by the desire to do justice by their students.

Accountability through recording has been a matter left to the professionalism and initiative of individual teachers and schools. As long ago as 1975 the Confederation of British Industry (CBI) had suggested that reporting to users had not consistently reflected employers' needs. It argued that

> ... although employers sometimes specify particular examination require-ments for certain jobs, what is generally being looked for is a particular level of ability, direction of interest, and a capacity for further education or professional courses. They are looking too, for such personal qualities as self discipline and self reliance, loyalty, integrity and enthusiasm. Evidence of attainment in the basic skills is also required.[28]

The variation between institutions raises the question of credibility, and it is in the context of national currency that the Secretaries of State in the DES Statement of Policy

> ... think it important that records of achievement, when introduced nationally, should be respected and used throughout the country by all who are concerned with selecting young people for courses, training or employment.

To that end they believe that

> ... the summary documents should be based on national guidelines, which would provide a common format, the necessary minimum of defined common characteristics and appropriate forms of validation or accreditation.[29]

The accountability dimension of records of achievement was taken up strongly by Mr Kenneth Baker, Secretary of State for Education and Science, in his address on the theme of 'The National Curriculum: Key to Better Standards' at Manchester University in September 1987. Referring to the assessment and testing aspect of the national curriculum, he said, 'Schools cannot just be accountable to themselves; they must also be accountable to the parents of their pupils and to the wider community.' Elsewhere in his speech he emphasised accountability to the pupil through the diagnostic value of testing and assessment. He explained,

> Rather than label children as failures, they should give them pride in their achievements and encourage them to strive for more. They are no back doors to selection – rather a means of satisfying ourselves that no pupil is missing out on essential areas of competence and understanding; that every child is reaching his or her potential; and that his or her particular talents are not being wasted or ignored.

Unfortunately, this child-centred view sits uneasily with his claim in the same speech that 'Each school will benefit by being able to compare its achievements with those of other similar schools.'

ACCREDITATION

The implications of this subject should not be underestimated. The fundamental questions raised by records of achievement about objectives, assessment, teaching style, school organisation, etc, suggest that accreditation, if it is to be meaningful, will require schools to undergo a fairly searching scrutiny of their teaching and organisation. In other words, it would not be unlike the inspections undertaken by HMI. However, there would be one essential difference; schools would probably be accredited for a certain period, after which the accreditation would have to be renewed. This matter will be discussed in more detail in Chapter 5, but, as the Government envisages records of achievement having an important role in the national curriculum,[30] it seems a strong possibility that accreditation will have a prominent place.

Summary

This chapter has attempted to trace the demand for a more comprehensive picture of students' achievements. It has suggested that this was partly based on the very limited amount of information given by examination grades. The possibilities and problems of the development of grade-related criteria have been discussed with a view to more detailed positive certification being the objective.

Developments in teaching strategies to involve students more in their own learning have been traced, and the benefits claimed from this process identified. The response of various organisations and groups to the introduction of records of achievement has been seen to be positive, thus welcoming the greater accountability implied in the change.

The roots of the accountability dimension are explored further with respect to students and employers, and the credibility of the record. The latter leads into an outline of the idea of accreditation and its implications. In the following chapters the issues raised above will be discussed in the context of practical implementation, bearing in mind the impact upon teaching, educational management and the needs of users.

References

1. Department of Education and Science Welsh Office (1984) *Records of Achievement: A Statement of Policy*.
2. Balogh, J (1982) *Profile Reports for School Leavers* Schools Council, Longman Resources Unit.
3. County Hall Dorchester (1987) *National Profiling Network*.
4. Harlen, Wynne in Cognitive development in the school years (*Ed* Floyd, Ann (1979)) *Matching the Learning Environment to Children's Development: The Progress in Learning Science Project* Croom Helm.
5. Schools Council (1981) *Working Paper 70, The Practical Curriculum*.
6. Hall, G and Derricott, R (1982) *Profile Reporting: Interim Report*, Metropolitan Borough of Knowsley/Schools Council Programme 2.
7. Coltham, J B and Fines, J (1971) *Educational Objectives for the Study of History* Historical Association.
8. Gard, A and Lee, P J in History teaching and historical understanding (*Eds* Dickinson, A K and Lee, P J (1978)) *Educational Objectives for the Study of History Reconsidered* Heinemann.
9. Hitchcock, Gloria (1986) *Profiles and Profiling: A practical introduction* Longman.
10. See Reference 3.
11. Schools Council (1975) *Working Paper 53, The Whole Curriculum 13–16* Evans/Methuen Educational.

12. See Reference 1.
13. SEC (September 1985) *Draft Grade Criteria, Geography* Report of the Working Party.
14. See for example Orr, L and Nuttall, D *Determining Standards in the Proposed Single System of Examining at 16+.*
15. See Reference 13.
16. SEC (1984) 'The Development of Grade Related Criteria for the General Certificate of Secondary Education, A Briefing Paper for Working Parties' Internal Paper.
17. *SEC News* (Summary 1987).
18. Rogers R (16 June 1987) The widening search for a measure of objective standards, *Education Guardian.*
19. SEC Press Release, 10 September 1987.
20. See Reference 13, section on Aggregation and Differentiation.
21. Dobson, Ken (1987) The issues are discussed in some detail in *Teaching for Active Learning – Teachers' Guide, The Suffolk Development* Collins.
22. Black, Harry and Broadfoot, Patricia (1982) *Keeping Track of Teaching* p 40, Routledge & Kegan Paul.
23. Burgess, T and Adams, E (*Eds*) (1980) *Outcomes of Education* p 12, Macmillan.
24. SCRE (1977) *Part 1, Pupils in Profile* Hodder & Stoughton.
25. FEU (1984) *Profiles in Action* p 79.
26. Op cit.
27. Goacher, B (1983) *Schools Council Programme 5, Recording Achievement at 16+* Longman.
28. Op cit.
29. Op cit.
30. HMSO (1987) *The National Curriculum 5–16, A consultative document* p 12.

Chapter 2

Unit Accreditation and Introducing Records of Achievement

Introduction

The purpose of Chapters 2 to 5 is to examine the issues and problems of implementation by looking at the experience of a school, which, for the sake of this study, shall be called Brant High School. Brant has not received funding specifically for the development of records of achievement from national or regional sources but is participating in the pilot scheme of the Northern Partnership for Records of Achievement (NPRA). In order that Brant's experience can be put into context, it will, where appropriate, be cross-referenced with findings in other schools both in the NPRA pilot and the nationally funded Education Support Grant (ESG) schemes.

The reasons for this approach are two-fold. First, the 'success' of an innovation probably has more credibility with practitioners if it has been achieved without substantially more additional funding. While Brant's LEA (which shall be called Winton for the sake of this book) has assisted the school by the addition of one and a half teaching staff, resources have not been available to it at the level given to those schools involved in ESG schemes. Second, the school caters for students in the 11–16 age range, and it is with this group in mind that most of the development work has been carried out both in the north region and nationally. With the exception of one school, the NPRA pilot scheme has focused on the 14–16 age range. This has not been from choice but rather because funding was limited and could not be guaranteed beyond August 1988.

The choice of age group was strongly influenced by the Secretaries of State objective in their Statement of Policy

... that it will be possible by the end of the decade to establish throughout England and Wales arrangements under which all young people in secondary schools will take with them when they leave school a summary document of record prepared within a framework of national policy which leaves scope for local variations.[1]

Given this intention the NPRA took the view that while it appeared logical to commence recording achievement with first-year students in secondary schools, it was important that experience was gained of the logistical demands of producing a summative document for students at the age of 16. These would include the task of bringing together assessments from up to 10 teachers to provide a coherent picture of a student's achievements. This decision was taken with the full awareness that the pilot scheme was going to coincide with the introduction of GCSE courses in September 1986 and the additional workload this would place upon teachers.

Before considering the issues arising from the introduction of records of achievement at Brant High, it is important to understand the nature of the NPRA initiative and Brant's place in it.

The NPRA development programme

The NPRA is a partnership consisting of 37 North of England LEAs and the five examination boards which make up the Northern Examining Association (NEA). It was established in 1984 to meet the needs of schools and LEAs which were developing new approaches to assessing and recording students' achievements. When it was formed, only seven LEAs were members and its growth to 37 can be accounted for in the popularity of its development programme. This consists of three schemes; two concerned with unit accreditation (Schemes 1 and 2) and the third being the *Pilot Study in the Accreditation of Centres for Records of Achievement* (Scheme 3) which covers the period 1986–1988.

The unit accreditation schemes

The focus of this book is Brant High School's involvement in Scheme 3. However, before considering this in detail, it is worthwhile briefly discussing the main elements of the unit accreditation schemes because Brant has participated in Scheme 1 since 1985, and each unit is a record of achievement in itself.[2]

The NPRA publicity leaflet *Giving Young People Credit* defines a unit as 'a short course of work devised by teachers and validated by the Northern Examination Association'. More specifically it consists of a list of outcomes such as skills, concepts, knowledge or processes which must make up a discrete, coherent programme of work that can be assessed. The unit can be subject specific or cross-curricular. To determine whether a student has achieved the outcomes, the teacher must offer evidence which has to show that specific outcomes have been achieved (see Figure 2). The evidence may take a variety of forms ranging from checklists or written tests to tape recordings or photographs. When a unit has been completed the centre (ie the school or college) will inform the NEA who will send in an assessor to determine whether the evidence offered matches the achievement of the outcomes. If this is the case the LEA will issue a Statement of Achievement signed by its chief education officer. The Statement will list the outcomes which have been achieved. At the end of the student's course the NEA will issue to the student a Letter of Credit. This will list the titles of the successfully completed units and be signed by the Chairman and Joint Secretaries of the NEA Council.

To participate in the scheme teachers may either write their own units or use units which can be selected from a bank of titles held either by the LEA or the local examining board. If he or she chooses to write a unit specifically to meet the needs of his or her students, the unit will first have to be submitted to the LEA for pre-validation before being presented to one of the regional validating committees for validation. The functions of the two committees can be summarised as follows. The pre-validating committee has the responsibility of ensuring that the unit represents a discrete, coherent, valid and worthwhile educational experience, while the regional validating committee considers whether the unit submitted meets the agreed criteria as laid down in its Rules and Guidance. If accepted the unit is then made available for teaching.

The difference between Schemes 1 and 2 lies in the fact that in Scheme 2, the centre, if it is sufficiently experienced, is allowed to pre-validate its own units. The LEA then validates them and sends copies to the regional validating committee where they are sampled. If the sampling suggests that the units are not meeting the NPRA criteria the committee can request a larger sample, and if it is still not satisfied can ask the centre to submit its units under the procedures for Scheme 1.

Principles and issues

The above detailed description has been necessary because embedded in the structure and organisation of the unit schemes are important curriculum principles. The intention is to give the student the satisfaction of achievement which, in its certificated form, normally has

---

UNIT ACCREDITATION SUBMISSION PRO-FORMA

SCHOOL: BRANT
UNIT TITLE: WATER AS A NATURAL RESOURCE
CURRICULUM AREA (S): SCIENCE

CODE NO.   WI097
DATE: MAR '88
LEA: WINTON

UNIT DESCRIPTION
The student will carry out experiments on water. He/she will show some knowledge of basic terms. He/she will make and test a model filter and use it to purify water. He/she will test water for hardness and investigate various methods of purifying water.

PROCEDURES FOR MAKING AND RECORDING ASSESSMENT
Assessed by the teacher using student-completed worksheet (1).
Assessed by the teacher through the student's written work (2–6).
Recorded on the assessor's summary sheet (1–6)

UNIT SPECIFICATION
All outcomes must be demonstrated.

OUTCOMES TO BE ACCREDITED	EVIDENCE TO BE OFFERED
In successfully completing this unit the student will have shown knowledge of	Student's folder of work containing:
	student-completed worksheet (1)
1) the meaning of the terms: sterilisation, pollution, softening, scum, distillation, de-ionisation, filtration, hard water and soft water;	student's written work showing details of the experiments performed including notes on the methods, results and conclusions on four investigations (2–6)
demonstrated the ability to	
2) make and test a model water filter;	
3) perform simple distillation of impure water;	
4) test hard and soft water using soap solution;	
5) test methods of softening water eg boiling, use of washing soda and de-ionisation;	
6) test detergent, sand and polystyrene beads as methods of removing oil pollution from water.	

Figure 2 *Unit accreditation submission pro-forma*

to be deferred until the end of the two-year examination course. This type of course assumes that students have the motivation and sustained interest to complete it. For many years teachers have questioned the assumption that this experience is appropriate for students of all abilities. However, the problem has been to find a suitable replacement, assessed and certificated by a credible outside body, yet allowing schools to devise courses to meet particular needs. The NEA meets these criteria. Furthermore, the Letter of Credit with its Statement(s) of Achievement attached list the outcomes achieved and are far more informative to users than a grade on a GCSE certificate. It will be remembered that in Chapter 1 a number of problems have been encountered in attempting a similar profile of performance for GCE.

Units, while initially devised with mainly the needs of lower-ability students in mind, are now being used with all abilities. Their flexibility on the one hand allows for a GCSE course to be assessed in unit form while, on the other, an area of the curriculum such as work experience can also be developed into a coherent teaching unit(s). They have improved student motivation. NPRA monitoring and observation by staff at Brant High has indicated greater student interest and desire to do well. This can be attributed to the outcomes being explained and taught as realistic targets which student and teacher can record as and when they have been achieved. Teachers have noted that attendance records have improved, discipline problems have decreased and student attitudes towards learning have been more positive than in previous years. These changes have been put down to students being more involved in the learning process through the discussion of units and feeling more valued as a result.

An important factor in sustaining interest is the awarding of the Statement of Achievement which has to be presented as soon as possible after the successful completion of a unit. At Brant this occurs after about four weeks which is the time required for assessment and administration. The presentation is treated as an important occasion and the response from the students, like the statements they receive, is positive. If outcomes are not achieved the schemes allow for a time extension. At Brant the need to move on to the next phase of the course, whether it is GCSE or Personal and Social Education, is given priority so extension is not allowed.

The unit schemes are essentially a test of teacher professionalism. Curriculum development skills are required to structure a coherent, discrete programme of work in such a way that the skills and knowledge outcomes can be assessed by provision of the appropriate evidence. Recording students' achievements is detailed and demanding. The traditional mark book is no longer suitable for the recording task, as the assessor has to be assured that the evidence provided by the student's work shows that the outcomes have been achieved. This relationship must be abundantly clear because the assessor's task is limited to this brief. It will only be by chance if the assessor's subject expertise coincides with the unit taught. Indeed, the scheme has been criticized on this count. The expertise of the teacher is therefore very important. In Winton, to ensure the credibility of units outside the knowledge of the pre-validating committee, the advice of subject specialists is sought.

The unit schemes have also been questioned on account of the absence of standardisation. Two members of the Records of Achievement National Steering Committee (RANSC) on a liaison visit to sample the work of the NPRA commented:

> The devolution of validation of work units to LEAs and schools highlights the question of standardisation: to what extent is it desirable or practicable to have certified statements of achievement that will enjoy parity of esteem among pupils and other potential users?[3]

This is perhaps to misunderstand the nature of unit accreditation which is to give credit for what students, as individuals, have experienced and achieved. However, what the NPRA must note is that if presumably informed observers are making this kind of observation, the task of educating 'lay users' is formidable.

At Brant High this is acknowledged as being crucial for the credibility of the schemes. It has been pointed out that the task is made all the more difficult because unit accreditation may be seen as being in competition with GCSE and other nationally recognised courses. One strategy which may assist in coping with this problem is to educate students with regard to the use of statements of achievement and letters of credit in job applications and at interviews. Outcomes compared with GCSE grades provide a more useful agenda for discussion between student and such potential recruiters as employers, further and higher education and Youth Training Scheme (YTS) agents.

The quest for credibility has been taken up by many teachers in the form of attempting to link unit accreditation with GCSE. As mentioned above, teachers have broken down GCSE syllabuses into units or modules as a means of motivating students and sustaining their interest over the two-year course. However, it is a much more difficult task to relate the successful completion of units to the achievement of specific GCSE grades. The GCSE and unit accreditation modes of assessment are very different, the former being norm related while the latter is criteria referenced. The demands on teachers in preparing students' work to meet the requirements of both assessment systems would be considerable. Even if this can be achieved the question must arise as to whether it is acceptable to have units of a different status; that is, those officially linked to GCSE grades and those which are not.

As indicated earlier, the popularity of the NPRA development programme has led to a rapid growth in the number of schools involved and units taught. This has led to administrative pressures within schools, LEAs and examination boards. At Brant High there is disquiet regarding the amount of paperwork involved. One teacher explained that he used between 15 and 20 units each year, and the record keeping together with the presentation of material for the assessor had resulted in a considerable increase in his workload. He suggested that some form of payment should be made, but as requests for additional payment for GCSE coursework administration have been rejected on the grounds that it is considered to be part of the teacher's role, funding for this work does not seem likely.

With regard to the examination boards, Scheme 2 is seen not only as an opportunity for teacher development through school pre-validating committees and LEA involvement at the validation level, but as a means of sharing the administration. The implications for the LEAs are considerable as Scheme 2 or some variant appears to be the obvious direction in which development will take place. They will have to provide the inservice training (albeit with examination board support) and the administrative coordination.

Summary

The following represents a brief résumé of the main points raised above:

1. A unit is a record of achievement accredited by the NEA.

2. Units can be subject specific or cross-curricular.

3. Unit accreditation can promote motivation by giving students feedback soon after each unit has been completed.

4. Units are increasingly being used with students of all abilities.

5. Unit schemes demand a high level of professionalism both in devising units and in the recording of students' work. Outcomes have to be carefully matched with evidence of student achievement.

Furthermore, if in the future more and more schools join Scheme 2, as seems likely, teachers will also have to take responsibility for the pre-validation function.

6. The absence of standardisation is not a defect in itself but, for its rationale to be understood, it necessitates considerable public education.

7. The status of unit accreditation in relation to established national courses such as GCSE and others has given cause for concern. Attempts to develop links between units and GCSE grades have run into technical difficulties and have also raised the question of the relative status of linked and non-linked units.

8. Students require training with regard to the use of units with users.

9. The administrative and inservice implications must be accepted if the popularity and effectiveness of the schemes are to be maintained.

Scheme 3 – The NPRA pilot study in the accreditation of centres for records of achievement at Brant High School

Before discussing detailed issues arising from Brant's involvement in Scheme 3 it is important to appreciate the principles upon which the study is based; a little of the background of the school itself; and the context in which the decision to join the scheme was made.

Figure 3 outlines the principles which the Partnership believes should be reflected in the pilot study.

With regard to the above, the NPRA Booklet for Centres and LEAs stresses that the principles are not criteria for the acceptance of schools into the scheme but rather are providing targets for participating schools to aim at. It is upon the basis of evidence that they have moved towards achieving them that the NPRA will validate the summative document. This evidence will also enable the Partnership to identify criteria for the future accreditation of centres which is the aim of the scheme.

BRANT HIGH SCHOOL – BACKGROUND
Brant has a catchment which consists of about three-quarters inner-city overspill, the remainder being well-established families. Job prospects in the area are bleak. Less than 10 per cent of school leavers obtain employment. The school is a mixed comprehensive and originally catered for the 11–18 age range, but with falling rolls lost its sixth form

NPRA principles

During the pilot study it is hoped to identify good practice in schools throughout the North. It is inevitable that the experience of the pilot study will lead the NPRA to reappraise its guiding principles. Nevertheless, at the moment, the following are the principles which both sides of the Partnership feel should be reflected in the pilot study.

(a) *The methods of recording achievement* should aim to:
- (i) be an integral part of the learning process and should arise directly from pupil/teacher interaction, in and out of the classroom;
- (ii) provide for all levels of attainment, within and across traditional subject areas;
- (iii) involve the student in regular discussions with the teachers and in jointly agreeing future learning targets;
- (iv) develop in students skills of self-assessment and recording;
- (v) encourage in students greater responsibility for their own learning;
- (vi) concentrate on positive aspects of a student's abilities, experiences, achievements and personal qualities, both in and out of school;
- (vii) provide statements which are meaningful to users and written in language which can be readily understood by all participants, eg students, staff, parents, FE, employers;
- (viii) produce statements which are readily accessible whilst having due regard to security;
- (ix) ensure that the final document of record becomes the property of the student, whilst retaining a master copy of the record.

(b) *The administrative procedures for recording achievement* should aim to:
- (i) provide overall coordination/management of the record in school by one named person;
- (ii) ensure that each student has one individual teacher with overall responsibility for his/her record;
- (iii) allow staff access to adequate in-service training prior to and during the course of pilot study;
- (iv) include staff with relevant experience and training;
- (v) allow for as many as possible of the teachers in contact with the student to contribute to the record;
- (vi) allocate adequate time and opportunity for team development;
- (vii) provide adequate time and opportunity for monitoring and evaluation.

Figure 3 *Extract from* NPRA Pilot Study in the Accreditation of Centres for Records of Achievement 1986–1988 *(Booklet for Centres and LEAs, March 1986)*

when Winton reorganised its post-16 provision in the central part of the Borough. A tertiary college was established to meet these needs. There are now under 660 on roll. For the purpose of the pilot study 156 students in six tutor groups were involved over the two-year period from their entry into the fourth year until leaving at the age of 16.

Brant is staffed on the basis of heads of upper and lower schools – an inheritance of the 11–18 era, and heads of year for each age range. There are approximately 48 teaching staff, eight of whom are on promoted posts above the allocated establishment of the school. This has had its implications for the management of the pilot scheme in that, while one of the three deputy heads is responsible to the head for running it, two senior staff share the day-to-day coordination. One is responsible for its development, the other for its administration. This method of delegating responsibility has been brought about by falling rolls leaving the school with a 'top heavy' management structure, and the head saw the appointment of joint coordinators as a means of staff development and deployment on a project which had to be seen to have status in the eyes of the staff. However, as will be seen later, these obvious merits can be partially offset by how these roles are defined by the individuals concerned and how they are seen by their colleagues.

CONTEXT AND COMMUNICATING THE MESSAGE

Gross *et al*[4] vividly stress the importance of the historical context in understanding the basis upon which curriculum decisions are made. The recent history of innovation at Brant is interesting in this respect. With regard to records of achievement the school was one of two selected by Winton to participate in a project aimed at improving the performance of low-attaining pupils in the 14–16 age range. The project was funded through the Government's Urban Renewal Programme for the period 1984–87. Approximately one third of pupils in the school's fourth and fifth years was involved. The school received additional staffing, resources and support from a central team. Records of achievement were an important feature of it. Student involvement was strong in terms of their contribution to reviewing, and a promising computer-produced summative document, based partially on cross-curricular themes, was produced. Overall the project was deemed to be a success.

Given this legacy it might appear that Brant had a firm foundation upon which to extend records of achievement to the whole ability range with the advent of the NPRA pilot scheme in 1986. However, the wider impact of this experience did not occur. This has been because staff did not accept that approaches which had been successful in the project were either appropriate or possible with the full ability group. The effect has been to leave the school with a small group of committed teachers together with the idea of the comment bank[5] and a format for a summative document. Student involvement in reviewing which had featured so strongly was not taken on by the subject departments to any degree. What was significant was that all departments had embarked upon the exercise of identifying criteria and expected levels of student performance. They had been encouraged to make this a high priority during a LEA one-session course organised to support the introduction of the scheme, and this message was later endorsed by the school's coordinators during a similar in-house event which they arranged.

Given this experience the following points are worth making:

1. Although a project has been successful in a particular school, there is no guarantee that this good practice can or will transfer to previously non-involved colleagues, despite student involvement in records of achievement being identified by the DES in its policy statement as being important.
2. It will be noted that the departments heeded the message of the LEA and in-house courses that the devising of subject criteria, etc was important and treated this task as priority. It can be said that the two inservice sessions had a greater impact on the development of records of achievement at Brant than a successfully installed three-year project, which had records as a focal point. In attempting to understand this situation, two matters spring to mind; how records of achievement are defined and communicated, and secondly, that staff for perhaps a number of reasons choose selectively those parts of the message they intend to implement as high priority. How much this is related to the quality of the communication as opposed to the implications for teaching style will be discussed later under subject specific recording.

With regard to definition, whether intentionally or not, the inservice providers communicated *records of achievement as being about the introduction of a system as opposed to giving students greater control over their own learning* which had been an important message of the project. The providers may have been at fault in this respect in determining that student involvement was going to be difficult to achieve initially, because of the role change required of some staff, so put emphasis on the subject performance exercise. This met the principles of the pilot scheme, had the advantage of being a similar exercise to that required of GCSE course work assessment, and was an integral part of the

NPRA unit accreditation schemes. However, while this strategy appeared to have the advantage of relating together and meeting a number of needs, the lesson to be learnt is that the *whole message has to be communicated or frustration may result.*[6]

For example, later the school was criticised by the NPRA for lack of student involvement. This forced the coordinators to urge upon the subject teachers a dimension that had not been stressed at the outset. One coordinator summed up the situation admirably when he said 'At first we set up a system now we're searching for a philosophy.' *The important point to be addressed by schools is that they have to repeatedly ask the question 'why?' as a vitally important component of its monitoring arrangements.* It is to the credit of Brant's senior management that this issue has now returned to the agenda.

References

1. DES Welsh Office *Records of Achievement: A Statement of Policy* (1984) p 2, para 8.
2. Further information can be obtained from the Joint Matriculation Board, Manchester, where copies of the Rules and Guidance are also available.
3. Unpublished report on a RANSC liaison visit to NPRA, 11/12 May 1987.
4. Gross, N, Giacquinta, J B and Bernstein, M (1971) *Implementing Organisational Innovations* Open University.
5. The idea and use of the comment bank is expanded on in Chapter 3.
6. This point is enlarged upon in Hall, G and Derricott, R (1982) *Profile Reporting: Interim Report* Metropolitan Borough of Knowsley/Schools Council Programme 2, p 44.

Chapter 3
Subject Recording

This chapter first examines the factors which influenced Brant's decision to introduce subject-based recording, then goes on to consider departmental approaches to various aspects including the development of computer-linked comment banks, student involvement and the recording of personal attributes.

A subject or cross-curricular model of recording?

Before considering Brant's decision in this respect it is important to clarify what is meant by the terms. Subject recording usually refers to the performance of students in relation to the skills, concepts, etc identified by subject teachers or departments. Cross-curricular recording, on the other hand, has two aspects. One, it can refer to personal attributes displayed by students in a wide range of contexts across the curriculum. Two, it can relate to a skill(s) which has been identified by two or more departments as a shared objective(s).

The school opted for subject and cross-curricular recording; the latter being in respect of personal attributes only. This decision was made in light of:

- the problems which might be encountered in extending the successful cross-curricular experience of the low-attainer project (referred to in Chapter 2) to the whole ability range;
- the management implications;
- the needs of users; and
- concern for the place of subject content.

With regard to the first point (which concerned the problems involved in extending the low-attainer project to the whole ability range), a generous student/teacher ratio had operated, only about one third of the age range was involved and the students had been taught by a small, well-supported team who had been appointed on promoted posts. The senior management was concerned that these conditions would not prevail for the larger student group. There was also the feeling that commitment to this practice was not widespread outside the small group of teachers involved. As indicated in this context in Chapter 2, the 'ripple effect' of a successful innovation can be very limited.

The management implications were also seen as presenting difficulties. For example, communication skills, which had been one of the cross-curricular areas recorded by the low attainers project, would have required recording of achievement over as many as 10 subject areas. Furthermore, agreement on criteria and their interpretation in a wide variety of situations ranging from art to English would have been necessary. The senior management's view on this matter was reinforced after a visit to a school in Clwyd LEA. Clywd operates a cross-curricular model as part of its ESG-funded records of achievement project. Students' communication, numerical, practical, physical, research and problem-solving skills are recorded. Not only did the logistics and staff development demands appear insurmountable but meeting the needs of users and safeguarding the place of subject content were seen as important considerations. It was argued that cross-curricular 'titles' were unfamilar to parents and employers and that they more easily identified with traditional subjects and what they stood for. (It could be said, of course, that subject content has changed considerably in recent years and that users may not necessarily be familiar with it.) Concerning the need to maintain the place of subject content in the recording of student performance, fear was expressed that skills which could be more closely identified with particular subjects such as chronology (in history) might not receive due consideration. As one of the coordinators puts it,

> From what was seen at Clwyd, our view is that subject profiles give more information about a pupil's skills than the cross-curricular approach. The cross-curricular approach appeared to be rather 'thin'.

The reservations expressed at Brant are mirrored and enlarged upon in the Pilot Records of Achievement in Schools Evaluation (PRAISE) Interim Evaluation Report (1987). Summarised below are additional points made in the Report:

1. Departmental patterns of curricular organisation in many secon-

dary schools tend to inhibit cross-curricular deliberation.

2. There are problems caused by diversity. For example, one school is trialling a 'cross-curricular abilities' grid of 14 items on which pupils and staff are asked to 'agree' assessments according to a rating scale (competent, adequate or has difficulty). Examination of the grid revealed categories, the meaning of which is not clear. For example, what is inferred by 'ability to concentrate' or there may be more than one dimension as in 'ability to understand and follow instructions'.

3. Gradations between levels of performance were difficult to refine.

4. Inner London Education Authority (ILEA) teachers initially had difficulty in building cross-curricular assessment into their teaching, possibly because they were more accustomed to recording knowledge achievements as assessed by examinations.

Against this background it would seem that the technical and organisational difficulties are such that the recording of cross-curricular skills hardly appears worth while, yet great value is placed on their inclusion. Hitchcock[1] makes the following claims:

1. Assessment of cross-curricular skills is central to the philosophy of profiling – it assesses across the barriers of subject boundaries, and, by assessing them, makes it explicit to teachers and students that they are important.

2. Developing cross-curricular assessment skills requires support and training. It is unreasonable to expect teachers to adopt a completely new approach to teaching and assessment without such inservice support.

3. Inclusion of cross-curricular skills in the teaching and assessment programme helps to encourage teachers to look at the whole person rather than the performer in a specific subject.

4. Acquisition of cross-curricular skills may have a far greater degree of relevance for many young people than the traditional subject-based assessment which has so often labelled them as failures.

5. An appropriate environment and opportunity for developing skills needs to be provided.

   In this way profiles broaden the base of educational assessment so that the picture which can be presented relates to the whole individual.

There is no doubt that many of the staff at Brant would accept much of what has been claimed above. But given a climate in which many consider that the introduction of GCSE and the national curriculum have reinforced a subject-based approach to curriculum development, and bearing in mind the obstacles cited, it is not surprising that cross-curricular recording has been confined to personal attributes. It is perhaps significant that both the PRAISE report and the third phase monitoring study of the NPRA Pilot Study[2] note that the recording in this area (other than that of personal attributes) is not widespread. It seems that little movement will occur unless quite fundamental changes take place in the way the curriculum is delivered in schools and there are changes in national priorities.

The introduction of subject-based recording – time and resources

The remainder of this chapter will be concerned with points arising from subject-based recording at Brant and the wider issue of time and resources.

After the school had agreed to adopt a subject-based model of recording, the departments held meetings to determine criteria, levels of performance and comment banks for the computer. The latter were deemed important because they were seen as a successful element in the low attainers project referred to earlier, although, as will be discussed later, reservations were expressed regarding their introduction. Possibly of greater significance was the fact that the computer was seen as a means of reducing the staff workload. Bearing in mind that the pilot scheme was being introduced during a period of teacher industrial action, the senior management was conscious of the need not to burden colleagues if it was avoidable. The use of the computer and the allocation of time for departmental meetings were seen as important elements in the innovation strategy. Winton had allocated to the school the equivalent of one and and a half teaching staff and this time was distributed to the departments to allow the development work to take place. It can be said that this arrangement was the unofficial 'contract' between the senior management and staff which enabled the scheme to be introduced, although it was generally accepted that time over and above the additional allocation would be required.

The point which emerges here is that even those teachers most committed to records of achievement did not see their introduction being successful without either additional staff and/or a re-ordering of priorities. This view is endorsed by the PRAISE report (p 87). Quoting the Leicestershire Profiling Group it says:

> Records of Achievement can only take place alongside a re-ordering of educational priorities of individual teachers, of institutions and of the LEA.

It goes on to assert

... it is clear from the reports (from individual schemes) that as well as a very substantial voluntary commitment on the part of teachers, time must be provided in which reviewing and writing up can take place – either by re-defining the working day, decreasing the pupil/teacher ratio or other strategies such as team teaching.

The report of the National Steering Committee[3] on records of achievement goes further and is quite specific with regard to remedies. It states:

...the experience of the (Pilot) schemes suggests that a school-based solution to providing teachers with this necessary time is vital to success. The most favoured strategy is to allow a permanent enhancement of school staffing ratios, rather than to use supply cover (with its well known attendant difficulties). A strengthening of ancillary support is also desirable.

It is perhaps inevitable that this conclusion is reached when the nature of records of achievement demands that schools undertake a curriculum review which encompasses almost all its activities. The time and resources dimension has been raised here because it was a significant element in Brant's innovation strategy. PRAISE fully recognises this when it points out, 'Critically linked to management strategies is the now widely recognised issue of time and resources.' In this and other chapters, aspects of resource provision will be discussed as and when they arise in the implementation of recording achievement.

Subject-based recording

This section is concerned with the exercise undertaken by the departments to devise a system for recording student performance. It is important to note here that an integral part of this task was to improve the school reporting system to parents. A number of departments had expressed reservations regarding the 'cheque book' style report which tended to give little more information than grades for attainment and effort, and a rather global comment that did not always mean very much. This development therefore had the additional incentive for staff of producing a recording system on which they could gain feedback in the short term. In fact the school report at the end of the fourth year was treated as an 'interim summative' document. It is therefore useful to have fairly immediate goals to aim at, not only from the point of view of teacher motivation but early indication of user response enables a review to take place.

With regard to the exercise itself, the first task was to identify the criteria for assessment. For many departments this was a new experience. They had been used to assessing on the basis of a grade representing performance in the subject *as a whole*. It assumed that all elements were implicitly covered. Now the task was to make them explicit. The problems they faced were similar to those encountered in the SEC Grade Related Criteria exercise discussed in Chapter 1. They first had to split the subject into its principal domains (or elements). As most subject specialists claimed that their discipline had a unity, this was seen by some staff as a backward step. This problem was to be found with respect to the overlap between one criterion and another. Examples of this were knowledge and understanding in religious studies and concepts and skills in mathematics.

Another problem encountered by the science department in partic- ular was identifying criteria which in its view did the subject justice. It had identified four assessment areas: ability to follow instructions, use equipment, observe and record results and understand experimental work. The recording of these skills was to take place in the context of a modular programme which covered aspects of physics, chemistry and biology. The dilemma facing the staff was that to genuinely reflect the aims of the subject criteria representing the 'content' of those three subjects of science should be represented, yet to do so would be an unmanageable recording task as they saw it. It would appear that the difficulty lies not so much in formative recording but in compiling a summative report which adequately summarises a wide range of achievements. (This problem is explored at length in the PRAISE report, pp 17–18, in the context of an Oxford Certificate of Educational Achievement (OCEA)[4] school using a 'process' model of science education to record skills without reference to the content or context in which they are demonstrated.) This matter is discussed at length in the National Curriculum Report of the Science Working Group, 1988.

The question of the number of criteria, which is part of the problem discussed above, has had to be faced by most of the departments at Brant. With regard to managing recording, some guidance was available from previous work done in the Borough.[5] Experience had shown that recording five or six criteria was manageable. If the number was larger the difficulties of overlap between criteria became progres- sively severe, as did the recording. Fundamental to this approach has been the need to gain consensus on definition. In the larger depart- ments this has been a demanding yet rewarding staff development exercise in itself. Gaining agreement between five or six people bearing in mind the issues raised above, and the fact that four departments requested additional time to complete the task suggests that inservice support in the form of consultancy might have reduced frustration and facilitated progress. This was not requested but the experience highlighted an important need which should be recognised in the planning of inservice programmes.

Related to the above but in a different context is the position of departments consisting of one teacher, or one specialist with non-specialists. Here the problem is often one of isolation combined with the difficulty of recording achievement on the basis of very limited timetabled contact with a large number of students. The head of religious studies remarked that he would have valued an opportunity to hear the views of others. His position is made particularly difficult with Brant being one of only eight county secondary schools in Winton, the remainder being Roman Catholic Aided, and, as the other schools were not in the pilot study, there was not the mechanism or motivation for the respective departments to be brought together.

Some departments such as history and commerce adopted the GCSE coursework criteria. They were quick to appreciate that GCSE coursework assessment was essentially a profiling exercise and could be combined with the requirements of the pilot study. On the other hand, the science department did not find this feasible and was faced with the problem of recording achievement with two frameworks in mind. The subject criteria for the pilot study were included within those for the GCSE but administratively the two did not make for easy recording.

Levels of achievement – teaching style and the objectives model

The issues of number, definition and overlap discussed above in relation to criteria also had to be tackled in establishing levels of achievement. In addition, it had to be ensured that the levels could be identified and assessed in the teaching situation. The implications of this were noticeable in the history department. A teacher remarked that the teaching of 'castles' would never be quite the same again. He was referring to what had been an almost intuitive style developed over years of experience. Now he had to make himself much more aware of assessment criteria. One Winton geography teacher summed up this change by suggesting that he had become more 'conscious of objectives'. On the one hand, this approach might be considered to be towards promoting better teaching, and certainly the attainment targets suggested in the national curriculum, which will be discussed in Chapter 6, could demand it. However, the question is raised, how much will this kind of structure inhibit flair in the teaching situation? Observation of Winton schools suggests that at present this is not the case, but the obvious danger must be borne in mind. Objectives should be servants of teaching and not a potential straitjacket.

Basic to this approach is, of course, whether objectives should be pre-specified. This was not an issue at Brant, but the PRAISE Report (p 14) quotes an Essex head of department as follows:

> He resisted pre-specifying what pupils should learn as a result of their experiences in drama because he was fundamentally committed to an approach that allows pupils the opportunity to analyse what they personally have gained from drama events. This will vary from individual to individual and will sometimes be unexpected.

In this case, clearly, pre-specification represented an unacceptable constraint. This criticism can be levelled at imposed models of objectives and the attainment targets in the national curriculum come into this category. However, most difficulties are likely to be encountered in those areas of the curriculum where teachers put great value on students being allowed the freedom to explore and interpret situations. The creative arts in such areas as painting and sculpture are examples.

Comment banks and the role of the computer

As indicated earlier, the use of the computer was seen by the school to be a key feature in the pilot study. Briefly, departments were asked to produce comments of not more than 52 letters (the maximum the computer could cope with) in relation to their criteria. Staff would make their selection, and the comments, prefaced by he/she or christian name, were then sent to the computer studies department. Here they were processed into continuous prose. The pro-forma completed by each department also had a space for additional comments which teachers might wish to make on individuals.

The response to this exercise was varied. For example, the English department produced for reading, comments which were criterion referenced and included cognitive and affective items. It reads as follows:

(a) Can read simple narrative.

(b) Can read material of a more difficult nature.
(c) Reads aloud fluently and with clarity.
(d) Reads aloud with expression and understanding.
(e) Can read for simple facts.
(f) Is able to read with more complex understanding.
(g) Is able to detect bias in a written piece.
(h) Can make use of reference skills.
(i) Enjoys reading alone.

On the other hand, the CDT department, among a number of others, wrote for all its criteria comments which attempted to represent the achievements of a wide ability range and were put in a hierarchy. The following are the CDT comments for Use of Materials and Equipment:

(a) He/she handles tools, equipment and materials with complete confidence showing clear understanding of their function and properties.
(b) He/she achieves worthwhile success in handling tools, equipment and materials.
(c) He/she has limited success in selecting and using appropriate tools, equipment and materials.
(d) He/she has difficulty in selecting and using tools, equipment and materials.

Six issues can be identified from these two extracts:

1. Is such variety acceptable?
2. Is it a contradiction to have negative comments in a record of *achievement?*
3. If a hierarchy format is adopted, can equal 'steps' between levels be achieved?
4. Is the 52-letter limit for comments a constraint? (This has been imposed by the computer program.)
5. Would the value of the comment be increased if it was put in context?
6. Are 'can do' statements a totally acceptable means of recording?

With regard to whether such variety is acceptable, the senior management at Brant considered that placing the constraint of standardisation on the departments would have been counter-productive bearing in mind the climate in which the development was taking place. Furthermore, it was felt that such a limitation would have inhibited 'creativity'. There is an indication that this approach is widespread within the pilot study. The NPRA development officer's investigation into the assessment of academic and practical achievement in the pilot schools[6] suggests that there is wide diversity of practice in this area, but indicates that a small number of schools are beginning to address this problem. While Brant's approach recognises the individuality of subjects, the PRAISE Report (p 14) raises the question as to how much diversity is acceptable and whether there is not a case for having local uniformity within national guidelines. The idea of subject attainment targets within the national curriculum may, of course, impose a framework which overrules local wishes. An important element in the Brant strategy is that teachers feel they 'own' the recording system. Later, how teacher involvement in assessment of the national curriculum will be discussed.

The question of whether it is a contradiction to include negative comments in a record of achievement has been a bone of contention at Brant. The DES document, Records of Achievement: A Statement of Policy, stresses the importance of the positive nature of recording. Certain departments, and in particular science, have made the point that it is unfair to users to omit negative elements and put the onus on them to enquire further. However, as implied above, a record ceases to be one of achievement if it includes evidence of failure. This should be made clear to users, and a means of obtaining additional information identified. Many schools in the pilot study, including Brant, have worked on the assumption that the summative document is replacing the school leaving report which generally did include negative comments. The whole question of users' needs will be returned to later.

The third point is concerned with how, if the comments are being used as 'achievement' levels in a norm-related framework, the relationship between them can be made explicit and the 'steps' equal. In the CDT example above, the comments would have more meaning if examples of tasks achieved at each level could be included. With regard to the question of equal divisions or steps, examples would assist in these decisions, but the exercise is very demanding and staff will require considerable consultancy support in writing comments which reflect this pattern.

Regarding the 52-letter limit for comments, the English department remarked upon this number as restricting and it does prevent the examples being quoted as suggested in the third point.

The fifth point – whether the value of the comment would be increased if it was put into context – is related to the third and fourth points in that comments can be construed as anodyne if they are not put in context. As suggested above, examples of achievement can assist in this respect. The history department at Brant has moved in this direction by exemplifying the meaning of the comment. The following is an extract from its assessment framework:

Criterion: understanding historical words and ideas achievement levels
(a) Can clearly understand and explain difficult historical terms and ideas (eg capitalism, democracy, laissez-faire and cause and effect of events).
(b) Can understand difficult terms and ideas (eg Free Trade, entrepreneur, Non-Conformist).
(c) Can understand a number of historical terms and ideas (eg government, urbanisation, railway mania).
(d) Can begin to understand simple historical terms and ideas (eg peasant, landlord, tenant, industry, agriculture).

To be fair to this system there is an opportunity for departments in the final section of the computer pro-forma to identify additional comments for inclusion. Unfortunately, the letter limitation is still present, and in practice most departments mainly used it to comment on disruptive behaviour.

The context problem has been approached differently by another school in Winton. Here, similar to Brant, comments from the departmental bank are selected, processed by the computer and put into prose form. The difference is that they are prefaced by a paragraph which describes the course content. Figure 4 is an extract from the third year report.

This format, I suggest, goes some way towards solving the problem. More than that, it is informative to parents. Parents' reaction to this style of reporting will be discussed later in the book. It is sufficient to say at this stage that the parents at Brant, while generally welcoming the new style of reporting, would, from their comments, have found the additional information of the course outlines most useful. The National Foundation of Educational Research (NFER) survey[7] of school reports to parents in over 800 maintained secondary and special schools (1984) strongly supports this view.

Six, 'can do' statements or similar wordings have the advantages of being precise and positive. However, in practice, some departments have concluded that they are applicable to a fairly limited range of tasks. For example, with regard to 'Information Finding Skills' the history staff considered that the following offered sufficient precision for decisions on student achievement to be made without too much difficulty:

- Can locate relevant books and use contents and index to find information without guidance.

St Edmund Arrowsmith Comprehensive School

RECORD OF ACHIEVEMENT

Third Year French

The third year course is an important foundation for the GCSE course in years 4 and 5. It is a topic-based course, with the emphasis on communication in a variety of practical situations that may occur, for example, during a visit to the country. In French the topics include:

(1) Talking and enquiring about things to do with France.
(2) Train travel.
(3) Staying with a family (+ having a meal).
(4) School life.
(5) Changing money at the bank.

More topics may be introduced in the Summer Term of the third year.

In each topic the four skills of Listening, Speaking, Reading and Writing are thoroughly practiced and it is within each skill that all pupils are assessed.

Rachael

Rachael is able to understand most of the important points of a reasonably long conversation, such as a discussion about train timetables. She makes a few minor mistakes, but is able to communicate a message with little difficulty including topics such as school subjects. She has no difficulty in interpreting the themes and relevant details in both short and extended texts. She may produce some minor inaccuracies but most of the essential information of a written task, for example, writing a postcard to a penfriend, is conveyed.

Figure 4 *Example of third-year report to parents indicating outline of the course and the student's achievement*

- Can locate relevant books and use contents and index to find information with guidance.
- Can find simple information with guidance from teacher and/or librarian.

On the other hand, the English department, after experience with this approach, concluded that there were so many 'shades of grey' in students' responses to an item such as 'Can write imaginatively and descriptively' that 'can do' statements were seen to have a limited use. It may be that this format is more appropriate to those subject areas which have quite precise objectives within their rationale. 'Can make a dovetailed joint' in CDT would perhaps come into this category, whereas in English, language development, for example, tends to be a 'road to travel' rather than a series of discrete terminal points.

Student involvement in subject recording

As long ago as 1979[8] a subject framework of criteria and levels of achievement was being used diagnostically with students in Winton. The advantage of this format is that strengths and weaknesses can be identified and new targets set. Students have played a central part in this process on the basis of one-to-one reviewing, or through doing self-assessment whereby after the explanation of criteria they assess their achievement in relation to the stated levels of performance. The teachers' and students' assessments then form the context for reviewing and target setting. This and similar types of practice have in fact been patchy not least at Brant. As an important aim of the records of achievement movement is actively to involve students in their own learning; it is therefore useful to identify those factors which inhibit or encourage this development.

The third phase monitoring of the NPRA Pilot Study[9] has identified a continuum ranging from teacher-orientated records through student/teacher jointly compiled records to student orientated records in its 31 pilot schools. Brant's position in terms of subject recording is a mixture of teacher-orientated recording, mainly with the more able students, and student/teacher jointly compiled recording with the less able, although some purely student recording does take place in the areas of work and residential experience. As indicated in Chapter 2, for a variety of reasons, a substantial number of staff viewed the introduction of *records of achievement as a new system as opposed to involving students in their own learning*. It was also noted that the following three factors perhaps accounted for this stance:

- staff attitudes were not conducive to introducing the student-orientated approach;
- the thrust of the inservice training pointed in this direction; and
- the senior management, particularly in light of the first point concerning staff attitudes, saw setting up a system as the pragmatic way forward.

These elements can therefore be seen as limiting influences. However, the 'system' strategy has its positive side. It starts from where teachers are – that is, assessing students' progress. It provides short-term targets such as reports to parents and the summative document, and these offer fairly immediate and tangible reward for their efforts. Evidence at Brant and other schools in the NPRA pilot study suggests that teachers are motivated by these targets. It can be argued also that the framework of subject criteria and levels of performance provides the necessary basis for constructive teacher/student discussion. Furthermore, the staff development value of setting up the system has been highly thought of by everyone involved. What has been said above is not to suggest that the strategy for introducing records of achievement is, first, to change the recording system then the student/teacher relationship, but rather to make the point that if the latter is difficult to achieve immediately, there are advantages in approaching this goal by first changing the recording system.

There is no doubt that attitudes are slowly changing at Brant. The senior management is now more aware of the benefits of student involvement as are some heads of department but, more importantly, requests are coming from the students themselves. This need for change has been stimulated by:

(a) the observed benefits of group tutor/student reviewing which will be discussed in Chapter 4;
(b) the comments made by the NPRA Development Officer in the course of her monitoring;
(c) feedback from various dissemination sessions undertaken by the school;
(d) the influence of membership of a Technical Vocational and Educational Initiative (TVEI) records of achievement Study Group set up by the LEA; and
(e) the network of pilot schools and conferences set up by the NPRA to encourage information exchange and mutual support.

With regard to (a), improved student behaviour has been seen as being directly related to the introduction of student reviewing. The combination of (b), (c), (d) and (e) has pointed the school towards its future priorities. The lesson it has learnt is that in the development of records of achievement, rarely does a school get it right the first time (and this pattern is reflected almost throughout the pilot study). Secondly, the need for flexibility in response to criticism is paramount. It appears that dissemination by pilot schools is an important ingredient in their development as leaders in this field. It is crucial that schools can respond positively and effectively to this experience, and in the section of this chapter devoted to the recording of evidence of personal qualities by subject specialists this matter is considered further.

To return to the constraints inhibiting reviewing by subject specialists; where there is the will to involve students the question is how can this involvement be integrated into the learning situation? First attempts in NPRA schools have tended to 'bolt on' reviewing sessions by identifying particular times of the year when they will take place. Experience is showing that this is unsatisfactory from both the teachers' and students' points of view. A head of history, for example, found individual reviewing with a class of 30 students difficult to organise in terms of keeping those not involved usefully occupied. The students for their part saw the situation as artificial and asked if lessons could be reorganised in such a way that reviewing could be integrated into lessons. The response of the teacher was to organise student group reviewing within lessons thus releasing him to take on a monitoring and consultancy role.

However, while this is one solution, it is generally accepted that one of the hardest aspects to change in education is teaching style, and many teachers would argue why this strategy was not suited to their situation. At Brant the questions of class size and safety have been raised by the science and physical education (PE) departments as constraints. On the other hand, the English staff have found that such an approach fits easily into their general philosophy and practice.

While changing teaching style may be problematic, it would seem that sharing course objectives with students would not be too difficult an adjustment. This is happening in the pilot study but the pace of change is variable. At Brant this need has been identified, and with GCSE course work becoming mandatory in almost all subjects staff are having to involve students more. It is possible that it is not a question of attitude change being required but rather a matter of communicating that the tradition of the curriculum being the 'secret garden' of the teaching profession no longer has a place. In Ontario this responsibility is placed on schools through its programme require-ments[10] as follows: 'To contribute to students' awareness of the objectives of the course.'

As was seen in the example given in this chapter, a Winton school has accepted this message in the form of the inclusion of the course outline in its subject report to parents. It will be seen later that the DES *National Curriculum 5–16* consultation document (1987) has identified records of achievement (para 32) as having an important role in the assessment of it, and in that context the importance of accountability to parents and other users is underlined (para 61). It can be argued that, if only in terms of a school's responsibility to its students, this is justifiable. The national curriculum will extend this to a wider group of users (particularly parents) and make it mandatory.

Recording evidence of personal qualities

The initial response to the coordinators at Brant to guiding subject specialists in this area was to point to the guidance given in the DES Statement of Policy (p 6):

First, they should attempt to give a fair and reasonable picture of personal qualities displayed by a pupil over a period of time at school, not an all-embracing picture of the pupil as a human being. Teachers should describe only how a pupil has responded to what the school offers and so confine the description to matters of which they have direct knowledge and evidence.

Second, the assessments should concentrate on evidence of positive qualities such as enthusiasm, enterprise, adaptability, persistence, punctuality, willingness to accept responsibility, ability to participate constructively in group activity and ability to work independently: the final document of record should not refer to failures or defects.

Third, any such assessment is likely to carry more weight if it includes concrete examples of what the pupil has achieved or experienced. The greater the extent to which personal qualities and skills can be inferred from such concrete examples the more valuable it is likely to be to users.

Fourth, the assessments should take the form of sentences written for each pupil, not ticks in boxes or number or letter gradings. Such sentences are likely to be fairer to pupils, more useful to users and less open to misinterpretation.

The response from the departments was to either draw up comment bank statements or to restrict their comments to subject skill areas only. Both approaches raise interesting issues. In the first, as with the skill criteria discussed earlier in the chapter, two kinds of banks are to be found. The English department offers a selection of comments without a hierarchy from which any number can be chosen, while such subjects as CDT, PE, religious studies, commerce and history, whether intended or not, suggest that there is one. For example, the English bank under the criterion of 'social attitude' allows teachers to select statement(s) from the following:

- Works well under supervision.
- Works well without supervision.
- Relates well to other pupils.
- Relates well to adults.
- Is sensitive to the needs and interests of self and others.
- Works with interest and enthusiasm.
- Can accept constructive criticism.

- Takes a lead in group situations.
- Displays confidence in a variety of situations.

On the other hand, under the criterion of 'participation and enthusiasm' in PE, only one statement can logically be taken from the following:

- He/she participates very enthusiastically in all physical activities.
- He/she is an enthusiastic participant in most physical activities.
- He/she is a reasonably enthusiastic participant in some physical activities.
- He/she is a pupil who shows little or no enthusiasm for participation in any physical activities.

The limitations of the 'hierarchy' approach are reinforced when, as in the case of Brant, personal characteristics are clustered under one criterion such as 'attitude to work'. An exception to this rule is physical education where, in addition to 'participation and enthusiasm', 'cooperation' and 'leadership/initiative' are recorded. This multidimensional format would appear to be more diagnostic than the more global approach of grouping traits under a collective heading.

Of course, it must be remembered that these recording frameworks were agreed upon by departmental groups who had to take into account what was feasible given the constraints of the teaching situation and this was a particular concern of subjects which had limited student contact such as religious studies; the need for consistency of interpretation, and this was a problem of large departments such as English; and the restriction imposed by the computer's 52-letter limit. This was particularly the case if the context of the trait being revealed was to be identified. As was discussed earlier in this chapter, context is an important ingredient for putting an achievement in perspective. The question of pre-specified objectives was also considered, and, when raised in relation to the affective area, points to the problem of matching comments to students or vice versa, a task made even more difficult at Brant where most departments had only identified four.

Those departments which chose not to draw up comments for personal characteristics, and they included mathematics, science and modern languages, raise the issue of the role of subject specialists in this area. One head of department considered this matter to be the concern of the group tutor. If this is the case, and subject specialists confine recording to predominantly cognitive areas, then this would only reinforce the pastoral/academic division in schools. However, if they do have a role, then the question must be raised as to how justice can be done in the recording of both the 'academic' and 'personal' aspects of achievement, particularly as the attainment targets in the national curriculum may command priority consideration.

The importance of the issues raised above was brought home to the senior management of Brant at a dissemination meeting towards the end of the first year of the introduction of the system. This turned out to be a significant event and a turning point in its approach, in that it persuaded the coordinator responsible for this particular aspect of the pilot study that computerised comment banks have limited uses. What is more, as indicated earlier, it points to the value of dissemination as a means of feeding back ideas with the system. Critics at this session argued strongly in favour of the 'evidential' approach outlined in points 2 and 3 of the extract from the DES Statement of Policy included on p 56. Its strength is that it states experiences and leaves it to the user to conclude which personal characteristics have been displayed. It has the advantage of putting personal achievements into context thus making them more easily appreciated by the reader. For example, a description of a student's contribution to an expedition to Snowdonia is likely to have more credibility than two or three cryptic statements of qualities. If this approach is the way forward then the resource implications must be accepted. Staff will require more time for reporting. There will be no place for the computer but the demand for secretarial assistance will be considerable.

Summary

1. The question as to which model of recording should be adopted is discussed, subject or cross-curricular? The management and technical problems are outlined as seen from the perspective of Brant and reflected in the PRAISE report. This is balanced by Hitchcock's views on the subject. It is concluded that considerable change is required both at school level and in national priorities if cross-curricular recording in its fullest sense is to be developed on a significant scale.

2. The strategy adopted for the introduction of subject-based recording is considered together with the implications for demands on teachers' time. It is suggested that additional resources will be required.

3. The problems faced by particular departments and the difficulties encountered in identifying and assessing subject criteria are discussed. The need for consultancy support for this exercise is highlighted.

4. The impact of an objectives model on teaching style is considered and its potential limitations noted.

5. The question as to whether there should be a standardised framework for subject criteria is discussed as is the provision of 'equal steps' within it and the problem of negative comments in a record of achievement.

6. The value of 'context' in relation to comment banks and the school report to parents is advocated.

7. The limitation and advantage of 'can do' statements are suggested.

8. The problems encountered in the involvement of students in subject recording are discussed.

9. The difficulties of using comment banks for the recording of personal attributes are explored, and the limitations of the computer identified.

10. The value of context and evidence in this area and its resource implications are noted.

To conclude, if the problems in recording personal attributes encountered by subject departments imply that this is not a feasible proposition because of the nature of the subject, staff attitudes or availability of resources, this infers that this area is the province of group tutors therefore creating or perpetuating the pastoral/academic divide. The PRAISE report (p 17) sums up this dilemma when it states:

If schools are in the business of fostering personal qualities and skills, should this be confined to the pastoral curriculum or is possession of certain subject skills (eg empathy) integral to achievement in subject areas (eg English humanities), and therefore taught in that context?

It should be noted in this context that the national curriculum proposals intend that *subject* content and teaching

... should contribute to the development in young people of personal qualities and competence, such as reliance, self discipline, an enterprising approach and the ability to solve practical real-world problems, which will stand them in good stead in later life. (DES *The National Curriculum 5–16 – a consultative document, para 68)*

It remains to be seen whether recording evidence of these important personal attributes can be effectively delivered in practice, when placed beside more cognitive skills which are going to be identified nationally in the form of the subject attainment targets.

References

1. Hitchcock, G (1986) *Profiles and Profiling. A practical introduction* p 145, Longman.
2. *NPRA Pilot Study in the Accreditation of Centres for Records of Achievement. Report of the third phase of monitoring of the Pilot Study.* Autumn term 1987.
3. DES Welsh Office (1987) *Records of Achievement: An interim report from the National Steering Committee* p 10.
4. *Oxford Certificate of Educational Achievement – a pilot records of achievement scheme comprising a consortia of LEAs – Coventry, Leicestershire, Oxfordshire and Somerset.*
5. See for example Hall, G and Derricott, R (1982) *Profile Reporting – Interim Report* Schools Council Programme 2; Knowsley LEA (1986) *TRIST Development Group Records of Achievement, A Discussion Document.*
6. *Pilot Study in the Accreditation of Centres for Records of Achievement.* Investigation into the assessment of academic and practical achievement and the use of unit accreditation in the overall record – A report by the Development Officers.
7. Reid, Margaret I (1987) *School Reports to Parents: A study of policy and practice in the secondary school* NFER.
8. Hall, G and Derricott, R (1983) *Profile Reporting, Schools Council Programme 2.*
9. See Reference 2.
10. Ontario Schools Program and Diploma Requirements (1984).

Chapter 4

Tutor/Student Reviewing

In Chapter 3 the participation of students in recording achievement was discussed in the context of subject teaching. Their involvement is now considered in relation to tutor/student reviewing. This is in line with the NPRA principle which aims to 'involve the student in regular discussions with the teachers and in jointly agreeing future learning targets'.[1]

At Brant there are six group tutors and it was agreed that they should undertake reviews twice over the two-year period of the pilot study. The main issue to arise from this decision was taken up by the PRAISE report (p 26). It asked:

Can the act of formalising the interaction between teachers and pupils diminish its productivity, or is some element of planning and formality necessary to ensure that time is used effectively and to convey the importance of teacher–pupil discussions?

The question being raised was whether by making reviewing an 'event', it detracted from its value.

Evidence from Brant suggests that initially students viewed formal discussions with some apprehension. The following factors can be identified to account for this:

- the review was unfortunately called 'an interview';
- it was a unique experience for the student in that, for the majority, it was the first time they had conversed at length with an adult outside their family circle;
- it was difficult for them to conceive the interaction as a mutually helpful experience when the tutor was seen as an authority figure, that is, he/she shared the discipline function with the head of year and was responsible for writing a character reference;

61

- some students were unhappy about their present relationship with a particular tutor on a one-to-one basis.

Underlying all this, of course, is whether the school climate in general is conducive to reviewing, and in particular is there conflict in the tutor role of authority figure and counsellor? The PRAISE report makes the point (p 25)

> ... relationships in one setting cannot be abstracted from those in another, and that difficulties between teachers and pupils outside the interview are likely to affect the interaction within it.

Phillips and Hargreaves[2] go further and assert:

> We believe records of achievement can improve and enrich the teacher–pupil relationship in secondary schools. Our own evidence suggests, however, that one-to-one personal recording and reviewing is likely to have only the most minimal educational value until more trust, openness and respect can be injected into teacher–pupil relationships in general.

The benefits of reviewing

Given the apprehension of the students and the potential constraints quoted above, Brant can be credited with the fact that tutors and students have claimed reviewing to be beneficial. The discipline role of tutors has changed in that, because reviewing has enabled them to know the students better, they now find they are handling problems that used to be taken to the head of year. For the same reason these problems have diminished in that students feel more valued and involved.

Indeed, the senior management see reviewing as a significant element in the reduction of behaviour problems often associated with fifth-year students. The tutors find themselves better informed to write the summative document than they were the character reference which it replaced. They see records of achievement as a means of strengthening the teacher/student bond and at the same time providing the link between the student and the school as an establishment. As the pilot study has progressed, tutor interest has increased. This can be accounted for by the fact that the role has changed from what amounted to an administrative chore in the form of register marking, etc to one of considerable professional skill, demanding co-ordinating and counselling abilities.

It is perhaps significant that the main inservice training need to emerge in Winton LEA secondary schools as a whole, with respect to records of achievement, is group tutoring skills. Even before the pilot study had been in operation for one year, the senior management at Brant had recognised this and arranged an inhouse training session to review progress. The importance of the newly acquired status of the tutor gave rise to their desire for greater recognition in the management of the pilot study and in the allocation of resources. The tutors were not represented as a group on the school's records of achievement steering group. This has been rectified and the allocation of additional staffing given by Winton was switched from the department to the tutors after the first year.

The role of the student

Once the initial apprehension had been overcome, there is no doubt that the students found reviewing beneficial. When it was realised that it was intended to be a helping relationship, they felt valued and cooperated. Some admitted that it was the first time in almost five years of secondary schooling they had had a prolonged discussion with a member of staff and welcomed the attention. There is no doubt the term 'negotiation'[3] often used for this kind of discourse is inappropriate. It assumes some degree of equality of status between the partners and perhaps implies 'bargaining' which clearly cannot be the case. 'Discussion' is more applicable.

While the students were quick to place value on discussions with tutors, success was closely related to their contribution to the summative document. This provided an important motivation for both students and tutors. The basis of the review is the questionnaire (Form A, Appendix 3) completed by the student (Form A was devised by Winton's TVEI records of achievement study group, on which Brant was represented). Assisted by the form tutor notes (Figure 5) drawn up by the coordinators, the tutor after the review completes Form B (Appendix 4) which includes the mutually agreed targets. Between reviews students are encouraged to record their achievements and experiences by completing forms which contain the details verified by a member of staff or other responsible adult. The items are then transferred on to Form B by the tutor for inclusion in the testimonial section of the summative document. The achievements/experience may be in or out of school, and it has surprised some staff that certain pupils who were not high achievers in school, efficiently and responsibly complete tasks in the community.[4] Thus a more rounded picture of

---

FORM TUTOR NOTES

RECORDS OF ACHIEVEMENT

THE INITIAL INTERVIEW

The purpose of this interview is to commence the formative process of collecting/collating and motivating the pupil to achieve success.

Opportunity will be presented to review each pupil in this manner several times over the two years. The information collected will be used to complete the section in the Record which relates to achievement in areas other than the academic. Also, the interviews and information collected should assist the form tutor to write the final testimonial.

TUTOR ACTION

1. Issue the pre-interview questionnaire.

2. Explain its use:-
   (a) an opportunity to contribute to their own Record of Achievement.
   (b) to assist the first interview.

3. Stress the need to record information:-
   (a) neatly
   (b) accurately
   (c) sensibly

4. Give the pupils opportunity to complete the questionnaire. (Form period-active Tutorial – PSE)

5. Collect in and review for major errors etc. Re-issue if necessary.

6. Organise a calendar of interviews and notify pupils of their date.

7. Immediately prior to interview review pupil questionnaire.

8. Select discussion points:-
   (a) Initial approach to pupil's contribution.
   (b) Pupils academic route.
   (c) Possible career.
   (d) Interests/activities or lack of.
   (e) School attitude as viewed through attendance/punctuality/dress.
   (f) Review pupil's own discussion point.

9. Record this information on Form B.

10. *Set a Target*
    For example: (a) improve attendance/dress.
    (b) issue a verification slip for one of the activities.

11. Complete Form B.

12. Pupil/tutor to sign/date review.

13. File interview questionnaire (Form A) and interview schedule (Form B)

Figure 5 *Notes for the form tutor on conducting student discussions*

the student can be portrayed for users. As one teacher put it, 'I never thought I would have the evidence to be able to use such terms as "mature" "reliable" "responsible" in students' testimonials.'

However, another teacher remarked that with the less able student she often had to 'probe' hard to bring achievements to light. This perhaps raises the wider question of disadvantage. For those students who may be disadvantaged in some way, they may not have the opportunity(s) to record experiences and achievements, particularly in situations outside the control of the school. Records of achievement could in fact disadvantage the already disadvantaged. The PRAISE report (p 13) takes this point further and asks, should authentication be a requirement? Quoting the DES Statement of Policy (1984, para 20) that experiences and achievements

> ... should be accompanied wherever possible by a brief commentary drawing attention to any special factors such as any limitations on the range of opportunities available to a pupil,

it gives the contrasting examples of the boy who helps his single parent mother at home and girls who look after and compete on their own horses.

It goes on to argue that to give any contextual commentary would be invidious in these circumstances and that:

> Placing out-of-school experiences on the agenda for records of achievement discussion, in this way, potentially increases the possibilities for differentiation and social control based on hidden criteria.

Clearly, this area of recording has to be handled sensitively by the school, and extensive knowledge of students and their circumstances is crucial. This is perhaps underlined by a comment from one of the tutors at Brant, who considered that in order to do the job effectively, it was necessary for tutors to have groups for at least a three-year period. She argued that over such a time-scale she could observe students in a variety of situations, and become aware of the context(s) in which achievements were experienced.

Motivation

From the students' point of view they were very much aware of the importance of recording extra-curricular achievements. They saw that they could be disadvantaged in the job market without this evidence.

As one put it, 'a record of achievement with not much to show from outside school would look puny'. There is no doubt that extra-curricular and community activities have taken on a different significance as they are now seen as important contributors to the summative document and inevitably job prospects. If these are important motivators, it must be asked if records of achievement increase the motivation of students in general. The DES Statement of Policy (1984, p 3) asserted,

> They should contribute to pupils' personal development and progress by improving their motivation providing encouragement and increasing their awareness of strengths, weaknesses and opportunities.

The PRAISE report (p 29) suggests that this is not apparent. It states:

> We have to say that we have little evidence of direct links between the introduction of record of achievement processes and increases in pupil motivation.

However, as the TVEI Coordinator in Winton has argued, if records are truly integrated into the curriculum, it would be impossible for this variable to be identified. To be realistic, it must be said that while it is an NPRA principle that recording achievement should be an integral part of the learning, none of the schools in the pilot study have fully achieved this aim.[5] Certainly this is not yet the case at Brant and the views of the students support the PRAISE findings. However, they do make the important point that they thought their motivation would increase if they were more involved in subject assessment. They felt strongly that assessment and recording should be a joint activity.

Student involvement in subject recording

In Chapter 3 reference was made to the problems being met by subject specialists keen to involve students in assessment. These were also mentioned in the PRAISE report (p 28). However, evidence from the Report on the second phase of monitoring of the Pilot Study (Summer Term 1987) suggests that these obstacles are being overcome. The report found that in the 12 schools monitored,

> ... joint reviewing was taking place with subject teachers as well as form tutors. In five schools, this was happening in *all* areas of the curriculum. The other schools were involving most areas of the curriculum ... [my italics]

It goes on to discuss the impact of reviewing on teaching styles. It suggests that most schools had moved towards a more 'pupil-centred' approach. The following are some of the examples cited as evidence:

> A recurring comment was that teachers were reducing their instruction time, that there was a basic movement away from the didactic to the open style. Others expressed this in terms of resource rather than teacher-led sessions. Indications are that lesson materials are having to be modified to accommodate more experimentation and experience based learning.

> Some teachers spoke of a more flexible attitude, much more oral work with the teacher in a 'different' capacity, no longer an information-giver but facilitator.

> ... since the start of the Pilot Study in several of the twelve schools, all subject teachers had adjusted to varying degrees, in order to provide clearly identified learning targets determined both by the teacher and the student and the two of them in review.

> The encouragement of a more participative approach, and more negotiated activities was something all the schools appeared to be committed.

It is perhaps too early to detect a trend in this area but what appears to be happening is that staff and students see the value of reviewing and are making adjustments to accommodate it. However, such potential constraints as safety, class management and control, class size and limited teacher/student contact in such subjects as music and religious education still pose problems which need to be addressed.

Implications of the role of the summative document as a motivator

Before leaving the question of student involvement and motivation it is worth considering further the implications of the role of the summative document in the motivation of students. As indicated above, contributing to it acted as an incentive to recording achievement. This must raise the question, however, as to whether it will have the same motivating force when records are introduced throughout the secondary school and the summative document appears distant. The school report to parents may of course be treated as an 'interim summative' but this might be only a partial solution. What will certainly be required is an effective 'training programme' for students so that they can be made fully aware of the objectives and value of personal recording.

Broadfoot and Baines in their Interim External Evaluation Report of the NPRA Pilot Study (September 1987) endorse this point. The Coordinators at Brant have been aware of this need since the commencement of the pilot study and produced an outline for students' use. This, together with communication through the tutors, appears to have been effective. The notes of a meeting of the school's steering group in December 1987 reported that the NPRA Development Officer, as part of a monitoring exercise, had found that the five student groups visited seemed to understand the purpose of records of achievement. In an attempt to improve communication and obtain feedback on the introduction of records one school in the pilot study set up a students' committee to keep staff and parents informed of opinion. Figure 6 is an example of their summarised response.

PUPIL PERCEPTIONS OF RECORDS OF ACHIEVEMENT – APRIL 1987

POSITIVE

1. Liked idea of discussion with teachers as they went along.

2. Records of achievement give more information than end-of-year reports.

3. Liked knowing what they were going to cover in a topic.

4. Liked knowing what they have learned and what they need to improve on.

NEGATIVE

1. Some of skills listed were *trivial*.

2. Records took too long to fill in and wasted lesson time.

3. Some records too difficult to understand and covered too much.

4. Some pupils felt they could not be honest in their comments about lessons – possible teacher backlash!

5. Time for negotiation should *not* be outside normal class time.

6. They felt the need to know more about records of achievements and what they are for.

Figure 6 *Students' response at St Peter's RC Secondary School, Orrell, Wigan*

Organisation of reviewing

To conclude this chapter, the issues arising from the organisation of reviewing will be considered. In the Brant form tutor notes (Figure 5) it asserted that there would be opportunities to conduct reviewing several times over the two-year period of the pilot study. In the event two reviews took place and none of the tutors, given the present level of resourcing, could foresee it occurring more frequently while they had groups of 28. The danger in this situation is that the preparation for the summative or 'interim' document can dominate discussions, thus limiting opportunities for setting short term achievable targets.

In Chapter 2 it was noted that one of the benefits of the NPRA Unit Accreditation Schemes was the facility to set short-term goals which helped promote student motivation. If similar opportunities are not to be missed then the optimum interval between reviews has to be determined. The PRAISE report (p 27) quotes pupils who thought that 'twice a term was "about right" since, as one pupil explained, if they were too frequent there was very little to add to what was discussed previously, and if too far apart things were forgotten'. The students at Brant would only go as far as saying that twice over two years (albeit reduced to 18 months by reason of the need to make the summative document available by Easter of the fifth year) was insufficient.

Both teachers and students would agree with the DES Statement of Policy (para 35) which asserts that reviewing should be regular and in Brant's case more frequent. Unlike reviewing by subject specialists which ideally should be integrated into learning, tutor/student discussions require quite specific time set aside. A variety of strategies have attempted to overcome this problem. They can be classified as either being related to changing the basis of reviewing or attempting to increase tutorial time.

With regard to the former, changing the format has sometimes been seen as desirable not only to reduce the time difficulty, but concern has been expressed about one-to-one discussions, although the impression is that it remains the predominant form of interaction. As indicated earlier in this chapter, students at Brant initially viewed the prospect as an ordeal. In the first phase, monitoring of the NPRA Pilot Study the Development Officer reported:

> Another school which had had many years' experience of one-to-one reviewing sessions had come to regard these as undesirable for a number of reasons. One major reason was that students found them threatening, whereas if they were reviewed in pairs or with a group of friends they found

it less so. Many schools have echoed this sentiment and are increasingly encouraging form teachers to review with groups of three students or more.

Another aspect is identified in the PRAISE report (p 48) and by Broadfoot and Baines[6] which points to the linguistic and social difficulties faced by students from ethnic minority backgrounds in this situation. For example, it raises the issue of the prudence of girls talking to male teachers and asserts there are added cultural problems for Asian girls talking to male teachers and possibly for boys talking to female staff. However, if group reviewing is seen as a means of overcoming at least some of these difficulties, it must be remembered that the group itself can inhibit individual contributors, and it will require, to be effective, the creation of situations where it can be assured that all will have something positive to contribute.

Concerning the time requirement, as indicated earlier the senior management at Brant, appreciating the need for tutor/student reviewing to have priority, switched their allocation of additional staff time for records of achievement from the subject departments to the group tutors. The interim report from the National Steering Committee[7] strongly favours this approach. It argues,

> The greatest need is for teacher time for recording, reviewing and discussion with pupils; the experience of the schemes suggests that a school-based solution to providing teachers with this necessary time is vital to success. The most favoured strategy is to allow a permanent enhancement of schools' staffing ratios, rather than to use supply cover (with its well known attendant difficulties). A strengthening of ancillary support is also desirable.

One might add that withdrawal of students from lessons and arrangements whereby impromptu discussions might take place have also proved unsatisfactory. With regard to the latter, it has been claimed by some staff at Brant that this has the advantage of teachers reacting almost immediately to a student's achievement or experience, thus capitalising on the freshness of the event. (Indeed, some students at Brant have complained about the long time gap between the achievement and the review on the grounds that due to its distance in time the memory has grown dim, and its value as a basis for discussion is therefore limited.) In practice this has proved difficult to achieve, largely because it has not been easy to match the availability of students and teachers, or always to find suitable accommodation.

Following on from the question as to whether reviewing should be a timetabled or impromptu event, is the issue of the discussion being planned or unplanned. The Interim Report of the National Steering

Committee[8] advises us that it is 'likely to require some evidence of planned discussion between students and teachers'. Initially at Brant, because the experience was new to the tutors, there was the tendency to overplan by following religiously the notes for tutors (see p 64). The outcome turned out to be a rather 'mechanical' discussion. However, as tutors became more experienced so reviewing developed more naturally. It is perhaps a criterion of a successful teacher/student relationship that discourse can take place in an uninhibited way, yet at the same time be working to a plan.

It is worthwhile at this point discussing the focus of reviewing. In Brant's case it is a combination of the pre-interview questionnaire completed by the student (see Appendix 3) and the verification form (Figure 7).

BRANT HIGH SCHOOL

VERIFICATION FORM

VERIFIED DETAILS WILL BE INCLUDED IN FINAL RECORD

This is to verify that ....

has attended/attained/received/participated ....

....

....

from/on .... to ....

Signed ....

Position ....

Date ....

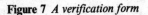

Figure 7 *A verification form*

The school had originally considered using student log books or diaries but discarded the idea after reviewing its experience of 14–16 low attainers project. The project found that it was difficult to sustain interest in this form of recording, and it could, in some cases, be counter-productive to motivation if it was seen as a chore. This view is supported by the findings of the NPRA Development Officer in the third phase monitoring of the pilot study.[9] Already in this chapter the question of disadvantage has been discussed with respect to those students who find that they have few achievements or experiences to discuss. These same students may be doubly disadvantaged if they have difficulty expressing themselves on paper. Some students have also felt inhibited about putting personal thoughts in writing, particularly if security and confidentiality cannot be guaranteed.

The main problems of the Brant recording system have been raised by the students. They have found 'chasing' staff for verification forms to be signed, frustrating. Although the pilot study is for the final two years of compulsory schooling, the students have been encouraged to record earlier events. This has not only caused difficulties in verification, but does raise the question as to what is the 'shelf life' of an achievement or experience in terms of its relevance to users. This has yet to be resolved as there is still no evidence as to what is the optimum period. They also mentioned the problem of access to forms and their storage. The senior management at Brant are having to examine systems which not only can cope with these demands, but look to the longer term implications when records of achievement are extended to the remainder of the school.

Access to records of achievement is an important strand in the development of student ownership, which is embraced by the NPRA principle that aims to 'encourage in students greater responsibility for their own learning' (see Chapter 2). In general terms, Brant appears to have made least progress in this area with respect to subject recording. In Chapter 3, problems were identified which the PRAISE report had also found in the context of the National Pilot Schemes, although earlier in this chapter examples were given of developments in this context in the NPRA pilot study. It may be added that there is an underlying accountability in subject recording to users and to examination organisations. This is not as mandatory in the tutor/student reviewing, and this is where most progress has been made. It is here where a sense of partnership can be truly developed.

Brant has achieved great advances in this respect. As one tutor put it, 'students now feel part of the act'. The students for their part are enthusiastic and feel valued, in some cases for the first time in their school life. The tutors, after initial wariness, are now on the whole very committed to the idea. Altogether, there is a corporate sense of purpose which is reflected in the cooperative climate apparent in the tutor/ student relationship.

Summary

1. The constraints surrounding formal reviewing are examined in the context of the tutor/student relationship.

2. The benefits of reviewing as seen from standpoints of tutor, school and student are considered.

3. The question of disadvantage is explored in terms of student opportunities to experience and record achievement.

4. It is suggested that the summative document is a strong motivating force, but in general there is, as yet, little evidence to support the claim that records of achievement increase motivation.

5. Examples are given of student involvement in subject recording and its impact on teaching styles.

6. The importance of communicating the purpose of records to students is stressed, particularly when they are introduced throughout the school, and the 'carrot' of the summative document is some distance in time away.

7. The organisation of reviewing is considered in terms of alternatives to the one-to-one relationship, time and frequency implications, and planned and impromptu discussions.

8. The question of the use of log books is looked at, and reservations are expressed, and the question of disadvantage is again raised.

9. A discussion of verification of achievements/experiences leads into a consideration of their 'shelf life'.

10. The importance of setting up systems which allow easy student access is put forward as an aspect of ownership.

11. The chapter concludes with a reassertion of the value of reviewing as a partnership with a corporate sense of purpose.

References

1. The Pilot Study principles are listed in Chapter 2.
2. Phillips, P and Hargreaves, A (11/9/87) Closed Encounters *Times Educational Supplement*.
3. The term 'negotiation' has its origins in profiling post-16, for example in City and Guilds of London Institute (CGLI) courses. It may be appropriate with students who attend voluntary adult or quasi-adult institutions, but a very different climate exists in the pre-16 sectors.

4. Examples of this can also be found in 'Records of Achievement at 16: some examples of current practice' HMI survey, DES Publications, Despatch Centre, Canons Park, Honeypot Lane, Stanmore, Middlesex.
5. This is expanded in the 'Report on the second phase of monitoring of the NPRA Pilot Study by the Development Officer' Summer term, 1987.
6. Broadfoot, P and Baines, B *Interim External Evaluation Report, Pilot Study in the Accreditation of Centres for Records of Achievement 1986–88.*
7. DES Welsh Office (1987) *Records of Achievement: An Interim Report from the National Steering Committee.*
8. See Reference 7 (para 54).
9. *NPRA Pilot Study in the Accreditation of Centres for Records of Achievement. Report on the third phase of monitoring the Pilot Study* Autumn term, 1987.

Chapter 5

Formative to Summative, Users' Needs, Management Issues and Accreditation

Introduction

This chapter is concerned with aspects of the formative–summative process and includes users' views, management issues together with a consideration of accreditation. Figure 8 and Appendix 5, the summative records of achievement of two students from Brant, provide the focus for the early part of the chapter. While the content is bona fide the names of the students and staff are fictitious. To be added to the back of the record are the students' achievements in public examinations and an NEA Letter of Credit. These the student would attach when they became available. The documents are presented in an attractive blue folder with Winton's crest prominently displayed.

Formative to summative

> It is a fairly straightforward task to produce an 'ideal type' of either a summative or a formative profile. It is far more difficult to combine the two into one unified system. The underlying philosophies of the two appear difficult to reconcile. (Gloria Hitchcock, *Profiles and Profiling*, 1986)

This quotation admirably sums up the problems of reducing the experience of almost five years secondary schooling into a summary document. Tutors, students, subject departments, coordinator(s), senior management and users are all involved (or should be). The problems revolve around the difficulties encountered in translating student achievement in all aspects of school life together with those recorded in the community into a summative report which does the student justice, and yet at the same time meets the needs of users.

THE ROLE OF THE TUTOR
At Brant the role of the tutor is a key one in that he/she has to write the

BRANT HIGH SCHOOL

Headmaster
T. BARON BA

RECORD OF ACHIEVEMENT

Metropolitan
Borough of
WINTON

Director of
Education
A. BOND MA

JOHN JONES

Further information about this
Record of Achievement
can be obtained by contacting
the Headmaster Mr T. Baron BA

Figure 8 *Example of a Record of Achievement*

BRANT HIGH SCHOOL

Headmaster
T. BARON BA

RECORD OF ACHIEVEMENT

Metropolitan
Borough of
WINTON

Director of
Education
A. BOND MA

NORTHERN PARTNERSHIP FOR RECORDS OF ACHIEVEMENT

NPRA

This Record of Achievement has been developed
by Brant High School with the support of
Winton LEA as part of the NPRA Pilot Study
in the accreditation of centres. The school
has participated fully in the Pilot Study, has
been closely monitored by the LEA and the NPRA,
and has adopted approaches consistent with NPRA
guidelines.

March 1988

NPRA is a consortium of 37 Northern Local Education Authorities
and the five Boards of the Northern Examining Association

BRANT HIGH SCHOOL

Headmaster
T. BARON BA

Metropolitan
Borough of
WINTON

Director of
Education
A. BOND MA

TESTIMONIAL

Name JOHN JONES

Attendance 169/174
Punctuality Excellent

John has been a pupil at Brant High for five years. He is
following a course that leads to GCSE qualifications in a variety
of subjects.

It is obvious that John works hard in all areas and has
progressed well across the curriculum.

In school John has participated in many activities. He has played
in a 5-a-side football team and represented the form on school
Sports Day running in the 200 metres and 800 metres. He also took
part in the javelin competition. He went on a Geography field
trip to the school cottage in Wales for a few days, which he
thoroughly enjoyed and where he displayed mature, co-operative
qualities. He has a role in this year's school play. He is
playing Jacob in 'Joseph and the Amazing Technicolour Dreamcoat'.

Out of school John plays football every Tuesday evening at
Prescot Leisure Centre. He has a morning and evening paper round
and for a month he helped on a morning milk-round. He is
interested in practical work and helped his grandfather to build
a greenhouse last summer.

I have known John as his form teacher for three years and he has
always had a pleasant, friendly nature. His attitude to school
has always been very good. He is a reasonable, helpful and polite
person. John is extremely good at getting on with people - peers
and teachers alike. He thinks for himself and can be relied upon.

John's persistence and effort should stand him in good stead for
the future. He is looking forward to an apprenticeship when he
leaves school. I am sure that whatever he has the opportunity to
do, he will do well. I wish him every success.

M. BEMAN

Headmaster
T. BARON BA

BRANT HIGH SCHOOL

Metropolitan
Borough of
WINTON

Director of
Education
A. BOND MA

CURRICULUM
PROFILE

Subject Area	Periods	Examination Entry
Mathematics	6	GCSE
English Language	6	GCSE
English Literature	4	GCSE
History	4	GCSE
Geography	4	GCSE
Biology	4	GCSE
Design Realisation	4	GCSE
Information Technology	4	GCSE
PSE	2	
PE/Games	2	

Total 40 Periods

BRANT HIGH SCHOOL

Headmaster
T. BARON BA

Metropolitan
Borough of
WINTON

Director of
Education
A. BOND MA

SUBJECT PROFILES

BIOLOGY

John handles apparatus and materials correctly and follows instructions accurately and fluently. He is usually able to make accurate observations, records information effectively, and can interpret data to form a logical conclusion. John works well in class and has a good grasp of the Biology syllabus.

He is improving all the time and if he carries on working hard he should do well in his GCSE

B.PYLE

ENGLISH LITERATURE

John can give a straightforward account of story and situation and shows an understanding of the basic meaning of texts studied with some awareness of themes and attitudes. He can recognise some of the basic features of the way authors write and is able to communicate and justify a personal response in a simple way.

John tries to the best of his ability and works quite hard in this subject.

N.FOREST

PHYSICAL EDUCATION

John is capable of learning new skills and techniques and occasionally displays creative awareness.

He is always reliable and displays a high regard for safety. John participates extremely enthusiastically in all physical activities and cooperates fully with all staff and pupils.

He can, if called upon, show the initiative to act as leader and spokesperson. Overall he has attained a reasonable level of ability in some activities.

B.FITTER

BRANT HIGH SCHOOL

Headmaster
T. BARON BA

SUBJECT PROFILES

Metropolitan
Borough of
WINTON

Director of
Education
A. BOND MA

ENGLISH

John can read simple narrative. He can read from simple facts and can make use of reference skills. John can write imaginatively and descriptively and is able to write simple sentences using basic punctuation. He is able to produce a well presented piece of written work.

John is able to contribute to a group discussion. He can relate personal experiences and can give a talk on a topic of personal choice. John is able to contribute to a formal debate and is able to ask relevant questions.

He is able to listen to others and respond appropriately. John can listen for more complex information and can listen to and understand instructions

He works well without supervision and relates well to adults. John works with interest and enthusiasm and can accept constructive criticism.

J.BROWN

MATHEMATICS

John has a very good knowledge and understanding of mathematical concepts and has good recall. He is usually proficient in calculations and is able to set out all necessary steps in a logical order. With guidance he is able to analyse a problem and apply an appropriate method to obtain a solution.

John has a mature and sensible approach to the subject and has worked well.

D.GREEN

GEOGRAPHY

John understands some of the ideas behind geography and is able to remember sufficient information to give him a satisfactory grasp of the subject. As a result he is able to study geographical problems and come to correct and logical conclusions with some help.

John's approach and attitude are satisfactory and most work is presented neatly.

Whilst on the residential field course John displayed a most cooperative and mature attitude and could be relied upon to carry out tasks with little supervison and he maintained a good relationship with staff and mixed well with the group.

M.BULTON

BRANT HIGH SCHOOL

Headmaster
T. BARON BA

Metropolitan
Borough of
WINTON

Director of
Education
A. BOND MA

SUBJECT PROFILES

HISTORY

John can understand a simple order of events and a number of historical terms and ideas. He can distinguish between primary and secondary sources, can note contrasts and similarities between two accounts of the same event and can begin to recognise that evidence may not be impartial. John can make an imaginative reconstruction of a past event, exploring some of the feelings of the people involved, and can write an account of past events in terms of cause and effect, using more than one source of information. He can locate relevant books and use contents and index to find information without guidance.

John always completes homework tasks, usually of a good standard and is usually cooperative and hardworking.

John has been working with more commitment this year — this should pay dividends in his summer examinations.

G.REDIMAN

INFORMATION TECHNOLOGY

John understands some of the principles of data processing and the relationship between the hardware and software components of a computer system. He understands some of the techniques needed to solve problems and also has some knowledge of a few computer applications. He understands the effects of computers on society and usually completes his work during lessons.

John has satisfactorily completed his modular work, however, he needs to revise his theory notes more thoroughly.

S.FINKLEY

DESIGN & REALISATION

John can communicate design ideas in graphic form to a high standard and is able, with moderate guidance, to solve some problems requiring creative thought. He produces an acceptable standard of practical work showing a reasonable amount of planning and displays some understanding of the subject but needs guidance. He always shows interest and is well behaved.

D.FLOWER

Headmaster
T. BARON BA

BRANT HIGH SCHOOL

ACHIEVEMENT AREAS

Metropolitan
Borough of
WINTON

Director of
Education
A. BOND MA

Achievement	Verified
John Jones plays football at Prescot Leisure Centre every Tuesday.	T.FOSTER Employee
He had a morning milk from 14 September to 19 October 1987.	C.MILLINGTON Milkman
John also had a paper round every morning and evening from 12 February 1986.	Shop Owner
He has taken part in erecting a greenhouse during the summer of 1987.	N.PARRY Grandfather
John is playing Jacob in the school production of 'Joseph and the Amazing Technicolour Dreamcoat'	R.MORRIS Musical Director
He participated in a day trip to Styal Mill for History coursework.	G.REDMAN Teacher
He participated in a Geography Field trip to the school cottage in Wales from 21 June to 25 June 1987	A.HENRY Teacher
John participated in a day trip to Croxteth Park as a biological assignment.	B.PYLE Teacher

BRANT HIGH SCHOOL

Headmaster
T. BARON BA

Metropolitan
Borough of
WINTON

Director of
Education
A. BOND MA

<u>CERTIFICATION</u>
<u>VERIFICATION</u>

students' testimonial component of the summative document (Figure 8 on pp 76–84 and Appendix 5). It can be seen that they summarise courses of contrasting content as follows, to include:

- academic achievement;
- school experiences and achievements;
- achievements in the wider community;
- personal qualities.

Furthermore, the tutor has the task of ensuring verification has taken place where necessary (see Achievement Areas on p 83).

With regard to academic achievement, it could be argued that the two sentences devoted to it in the testimonial do not do it justice. However, the summarising role is difficult in this instance in that the subject profiles (pp 80–82 and Appendix 5) illustrate a variety of approaches, making a brief informative summary of a wide range of achievements extremely difficult. The point at issue is whether subject recording should be standardised to facilitate the tutor's task and make the academic element more illuminating. It was indicated in Chapter 3 that it had been the policy of the senior management at Brant to allow individual departments freedom to develop recording within a broad framework and that it would have been counter-productive at that stage to impose or even attempt to gain agreement on a standard model. The Third Phase Monitoring of the NPRA pilot study notes that schools are now recognising this as an urgent need and a major challenge. Clearly, to satisfy the requirements of subjects with such different characteristics as science and religious education demands considerable skill and compromise which may not always be acceptable (see, for example, the difficulties encountered by Brant's science department in Chapter 3 and the PRAISE report, p 18).

Brevity – student ownership and users' needs

Underlying this exercise, and indeed the whole summative record, is of course the question of brevity. It will be dealt with here but it is a recurring theme. It is related to the issue of who the record is for, the student or to meet the needs of users such as employers. On the one hand, the DES Statement of Policy asserts, 'The Secretaries of State think it important that records of achievement, when introduced nationally, should be respected and used throughout the country by all who are concerned with selecting young people for courses training or employment' (para 31); and goes on to propose (para 40) that records 'should become the property of the pupil'. Indeed, the latter point is a logical conclusion to the formative process, which, as we have seen, aims at encouraging students, through the medium of the recording/reviewing process, to 'own' their learning.

With regard to the former, the question of brevity is important and may be in conflict with the concept of student ownership and the notion of involvement in its compilation. For example, the Manchester Chamber of Commerce and Industry (MCCI), which claims to be the 'biggest association of businesses in the North West' (of England),[1] makes it quite clear: 'The summative document should be limited to one piece of paper.'[2] A similar view is expressed by the Wigan Records of Achievement Project Employer Liaison Sub-Group.[3] A survey of 60 Essex employers[4] is more generous in recommending that the length should be five pages. It stated: 'If it is longer it will not be read. If it is shorter it will not be considered credible.' Given these constraints (yet bearing in mind that students, as indicated in Chapter 4, are strongly motivated by the summative document's value to users), it will be seen that there is a tension between the notion of student ownership and the needs of users. The Essex survey also concluded:

> The pupil is the prime user and owner of the record of achievement. Employers are one of a number of important *but secondary users* together with parents and Further/Higher education staff responsible for course selection. [My italics]

If this is the case then employer demands for brevity and the primacy of the student may be difficult to reconcile.

To return to the role of the tutor, with regard to the school experiences and achievements, and to the achievements in the wider community components of the summative document, time from the additional staff allocation made available by Winton is provided for discussion with students to consider draft ideas for the testimonial (see p 78 and Appendix 5). The matters for consideration include the selection of items, their verification and their relevance. Choice can be difficult in that a large number of items may be offered, and the student may wish to include them all only to be told 'an employer won't have time to read all that'. This must be very disillusioning, and contrary to the spirit of records of achievement but exemplifies the problem of ownership raised above. On the other hand, the discussion may be problematic because the student considers he or she has little to record, perhaps highlighting the issue of disadvantage discussed in Chapter 4. In this situation the tutor has to aid the student's memory and this cannot be done without an extensive knowledge of the student and his or her background; thus reinforcing the point made by one of the Brant tutors in Chapter 4, regarding the need to know a student over a three-year period.

Students require tutor support if verification is to be facilitated. The 'paper chase' referred to by students in Chapter 4 is an acknowledgement that teachers are busy people and may not have data readily at hand, particularly if the event occurred some time ago, to verify achievements/experiences. Outside the school, the problem tends to be different in that individuals/organisations may not fully appreciate its importance to the student. In this case the broader matter of communicating the value of records to the community as a whole is raised, and that is only in its infancy at Brant and elsewhere. With regard to relevance, the age of the achievement/experience may be of significance. The question of 'shelf life' was referred to in Chapter 4 but at present there appears to be little evidence from users as to when an achievement ceases to be relevant.

Concerning personal qualities, the tutor's comments in the testimonial (see p 78 and Appendix 5) are based on his/her summary of achievements both academic and non-academic. In Chapter 3 the importance of evidence in this context was stressed and while this is specifically provided for extra-curricular and community activities, in the subject profiles, comments tend to be limited to skill acquisition in the subject without relating them to particular achievements/experiences. A notable exception is the final paragraph of the geography component. This situation is a reflection of the discussion in Chapter 3 which pointed to the mixed views of subject departments, with regard to commenting on the display of personal qualities. However, this contributes to making the summarising task of the tutors even more difficult, and their concern for consistency in this area has been voiced to Brant's senior management. This, together with the standardisation of the subject contribution referred to above, is clearly an important priority.

Some reflections of the subject departments

At a meeting of Brant's pilot study steering group in June 1988, subject specialists reviewed their contribution to the summative document and many of the issues raised in Chapter 3 were discussed. In particular, concern was expressed about the computerised subject profile (pp 80–82 and Appendix 5). It was agreed that the selected comments did not read well in narrative form. Some dissatisfaction was expressed that they tended to be anodyne, and a decision was taken that the comment banks should be reviewed to become 'expression banks'. Clearly, there was the recognition that there was room for improvement, and the computer department offered individual assistance in reviewing comment bank construction and paragraphing.

What appears to be emerging here is very much in line with the DES Interim Report.[5] It states:

> Many schemes are investing resources – both capital and clerical/ancillary staff – in the use of IT support. So far, ambitions in this respect have exceeded reality. Computers are a good servant but a limiting master.

A solution to Brant's problem is urgent, because, if it cannot be satisfactorily resolved, an alternative to the use of the computer will have to be devised with its obvious teacher time and secretarial implications. It will be remembered that computerisation was originally part of Brant's senior management strategy in 'selling' records of achievement to the staff on the basis that it would reduce the anticipated workload. If this has to be abandoned, Winton should recognise that this is the experience of a pilot study, and judged alongside the many benefits identified in the foregoing chapters, is worthy of additional resourcing.

Concern was also expressed regarding the need for context. In Chapter 3 an example was cited of a Winton school (Figure 4) which had included a course description to give relevance to the achievements of its students. The staff now regretted that this approach had not been adopted at Brant. The discussion revealed yet again the tension between doing justice by the student and meeting users' needs. On the one hand, it was felt that it was not a fair portrait of the subject or gave an inadequate picture of student achievement. On the other, it was argued that to include such additional information would increase the size of the document considerably, and this would inhibit it being read by users. The matter was not resolved but a practical point should be borne in mind; in Winton less than 10 per cent of school-leavers obtain employment so the employer category of user is very much in the minority. It could also be said that a subject course description should be included because the DES Statement of Policy asserts that 'expected (examination) grades should not be included in a record of achievement' (para 24), and this would be in their place. It would not be in the students' interests if expected examination grades were shown, bearing in mind that it is likely that the record of achievement will be issued before the main public examinations are completed.

The students' contribution

A theme that has been prominent in this chapter so far has been the tension between student ownership, and all that is implied by it, and the needs of users. This section looks at two other aspects – the presentation of the student contribution and the students' use of the summative document.

At Brant the students' contribution is to be found in the testimonial along with the verification statements in the achievement areas (see pp 78, 83–84 and Appendix 5). It is compiled by the tutor after discussion with student. However, some employers in the Essex survey and also members of MICC have indicated that it would be more informative about the individual if it was completed in the students' handwriting or by using a word processor, and was separate from the tutor's contribution. From the users' point of view it would be an opportunity to assess how an individual presents himself. On the other hand, it might penalise some students whose strengths may not be in this area. The Third Phase Monitoring of the NPRA Pilot Study found that staff had mixed views on this subject, and it is probably only with experience that an accepted form will emerge. It is likely to be bound up with the general credibility of records of achievement which will inevitably take time to develop as the gradual introduction of the assessment of the national curriculum finds its place in summative documents.

In Chapter 4 reference was made to the training given to students in terms of communicating the purposes of records of achievement and their role. Similarly, Burgess and Adams[6] have emphasised its importance and have given practical advice to them in this respect. However, there is only limited evidence[7] of students having 'used' records with users; but what is emerging is the recognition that they will require training. The Interim Report of the Wigan Employer Liaison Sub-Group asks 'Would students be educated in the appropriate use of such a document?' This concern is shared at Brant where training is seen as fundamental to students deriving full benefit from the concept of ownership.

The summative document is seen as the agenda for the interview. Unfortunately this immediately gives rise to the question – On what basis does the user invite the candidate for interview? If it is the application form, then the record of achievement may not play a part in the selection procedure. If the record of achievement accompanies the application form, it may not be read for reasons of length referred to above. Furthermore, if applicants are applying for a number of jobs or courses there is the practical problem of cost and time for the student

89

viding copies of a high standard of presentation. All the
the NPRA pilot study suggests that schools are making
to produce a document of high physical quality.
in many cases would detract from this.

Clearly, this points to the need for employers to identify where they
see the place of records of achievement in their recruitment procedures.
For example, a recommendation from the Essex Group is that

> Employers should indicate when they would like to see records of
> achievement by stating so in advertisements, through careers officers or
> employment agencies.[8]

This, of course, assumes that records of achievement are understood. A
comment from a careers officer in Winton perhaps puts the situation in
perspective. He said:

> When you're talking about records to employers you must remember a
> sizeable number didn't understand CSE, and, as GCSE is far more
> significant in their eyes, a prime objective must be to communicate its
> intention. To expect them immediately to accept records which are far more
> than certification is optimistic.

It is fair to say, however, that schools, careers officers, etc have only just
begun to communicate the value of records of achievement and,
although the Confederation of British Industry (CBI) supports the
idea[9] there is obviously much work to be done both locally and
nationally. However, if the above would appear to paint a pessimistic
picture, the response from the Wigan, MICC and Essex groups is
generally very positive and supportive.

Composition of the summative document

There is considerable agreement between the three employer groups
about the composition of the summative document, and Brant's record
of achievement broadly meets their criteria. However, they do make
observations regarding negative comments, objectivity, consistency
and standardisation and these are now discussed below.

Negative comments

It is on this issue that there is considerable agreement between
employers. They[10] argue that to gain a full picture of an applicant,
strengths and limitations must be revealed. It will be remembered in

Chapter 3 that the science department at Brant had adopted a similar approach, and the point was made that the summative document would cease to be a record of achievement if failings were recorded. It was also mentioned that if further information was required beyond what was contained in the record then the onus should be on the user to obtain it from the school.

The three employer groups referred to do not find this acceptable. The MICC asserts that education views lack of ability as failure and employers are not so judgemental as they have work for all levels of ability. Their emphasis is on employability rather than achievement. The schools for their part would probably make the point that it does nothing for a student's esteem if all a record of achievement does is to remind him or her of his or her failings. It would do little to encourage ownership or motivation. As the Interim Report of the national pilot schemes[11] endorses the DES Statement of Policy that the summative document should concentrate on positive achievements (para 13), it would appear that there is a direct conflict of view. How this will be resolved is unclear, but, as there are many elements in the record of achievement that users find attractive, it would seem that the interests of schools, students and users must be accommodated.

The Essex group see a way through the impasse by making the confidential reports, often requested from schools, open to students thus giving them access to negative comments about themselves. Another suggestion made was that comments about weaknesses should have a 'shelf life' of perhaps one year, because young school-leavers frequently develop rapidly in a working environment, and negative comments can become irrelevant very quickly. No matter how this problem is tackled, this is a national issue which should be addressed when the Records of Achievement National Steering Committee (RANSC) prepare national guidelines on the basis of the experience of the national pilot schemes.

Objectivity, consistency and standardisation

The Wigan and Essex Groups both ask for these three elements to be applied to the content of the record of achievement. Objectivity is the particular concern of the Essex Group. Probably with good cause, they express concern at the statement 'Can formulate a possible solution to a problem in science' under the Problem Solving Ability heading[12] which is neither specific nor includes precise context. However, with regard to the general principle of objectivity, it could be argued that the only available data of that nature is obtained from objective tests. Such instruments can only assess a very limited part of the curriculum, and to rely solely on this form of reporting would not do justice either to the student or the curriculum. Much of the information derived from school assessment is subjective because the criteria are largely assessed by instruments constructed by individuals, which have no national reliability or validity in most cases.

These considerations though should not detract from the general point that users have the right to expect that judgements are made on the basis of achievements identified in terms of specific criteria, backed up by evidence and/or context. This is an implicit part of the accountability dimension referred to in Chapter 1, and highlighted again by the national curriculum assessment procedures which will be discussed in Chapter 6.

The need for consistency is pointed out by the Essex and Wigan Groups. This includes departments adopting similar approaches to recording comparable summative formats, and Wigan go as far as suggesting that there should be some consistency in approaches to tutor/student reviewing. With regard to departmental recording, the suggestion, while not spelt out, appears to be in line with the problem highlighted in Chapter 3. Here the question of giving freedom for individual department development was considered *vis-à-vis* the need for common procedures. While difficulties from the school's point of view were recognised, the point was made that schools in the NPRA pilot study acknowledged that coherent policies were required in this respect and were working towards this end. This may be interpreted as a move towards some form of standardisation of reporting achievement which would appeal to many employers.[13] Of course, as was touched upon in Chapter 3, a standardised form may be imposed with the introduction of attainment targets as part of the national curriculum. This will be considered further in Chapter 6.

The response of post-16 institutions

In the discussion of users' needs so far, employers have been the focus. This section considers the perspective of post-16 institutions and parents.

POST-16 INSTITUTIONS

In Chapter 1 the pioneering role of such bodies as the FEU, RSA, B/TEC and CGLI in introducing profiles into post-16 education was recognised. It is therefore surprising and disappointing to find that school records of achievement have still to find full acceptance in FE.

At Brant the response of the principal post-16 institution receiving its students was not encouraging, and the other tertiary institution in Winton pointed out that its recruitment arrangements are well under way before the summative document is awarded in March. This situation appears to be not uncommon. At the NPRA conference of representatives from pilot schools and almost all northern LEAs at Durham in December 1987, post-16 education was compared unfavourably with employers' response to records of achievement.

However, the problem is being addressed through TVEI which spans the 14–18 age range. Records of achievement are a mandatory part of this project, and the Winton TVEI records of achievement study group is focusing its attention on this issue. Curriculum continuity between sectors in education has always been a problematic area, and is particularly difficult post-16 where there is such a range of provision available. However, as TVEI reaches the 16–18 age group, and post-16 institutions are confronted with the task of reviewing their recording procedures, the climate is likely to be more conducive not only to viewing records of achievement positively in terms of individual's needs but to be taken into account in the broader task of curriculum planning.

Parents' views

Probably one of the most rewarding aspects of the use of records of achievement has been the response of parents. Winton has a history of involving them going back to 1979. As indicated in Chapter 3, changing the report to parents provided a tangible objective for staff, and the development of records of achievement originated from the desire to move from the style of reporting which provided nothing more than grades for effort and attainment accompanied by a comment. However, while motivating staff it also fulfilled the role of improving the school's accountability to parents. For too long reporting to parents has been rudimentary, doing justice neither to them nor the students. The national curriculum seeks to put this right and this will be discussed in Chapter 6.

To identify the benefits to be derived from more informative reporting, a discussion of early work in Winton will perhaps indicate its attractions and potential pitfalls. A number of Winton schools went through the process described in Chapter 3; that is, subject departments identified criteria in terms of 'levels' of achievement and re-designed their school reports accordingly (see for example Figure 4). The objectives of this exercise were as follows:

- To give parents more information about students' achievements.
- To provide an agenda for discussion between parents, staff and students.
- To aid diagnosis of students' achievements, thus presenting the opportunity for collaboration in the setting of targets for the student.

An essential part of this strategy is an arrangement whereby parents' evenings are used as the means for discussing the school report. Many schools despatch the report home by the student or by post, but in Winton an increasing number use parents' evenings for this purpose. Attendance varies but in the variety of schools I have attended 70 to 80 per cent of students have had parental representation. Winton's director of education sees this development as an important aspect of the Borough's aim to promote school–community links. Involving parents in this way aims at giving them the opportunity to share in the 'ownership' of learning with students and teachers.

GIVING PARENTS MORE INFORMATION ABOUT STUDENTS' ACHIEVEMENTS

The strong impression gained was that additional information was very welcome. In contrast to the employers, length was not a major consideration. However, the question of language was raised. Often the problem of communicating a document written in 'professional' language to a 'lay' audience emerges. A deputy head, who, in outlining the new system to parents, used terms such as 'curve of distribution', soon lost his audience. This difficulty perhaps highlights the predicament of records of achievement in general. They are multi-user documents and therefore must communicate to a variety of audiences. It also emphasises the importance that schools and LEAs must attach to the communication task.

Schools are becoming aware of this and are devising strategies to achieve it. One NPRA school in the pilot study has set up a parents' group,[14] while another in the East Midlands Records of Achievement Project (EMRAP) organised an event entitled 'An evening for active parents or an active evening for parents?' The aim of this exercise was to introduce the idea of positive approaches to recording achievement through the medium of the construction of towers by the participants using paper, adhesive tape and scissors.[15] This simulation attempts to draw attention to different recording methods, but emphasises the merits of the school's involvement with EMRAP as one of the DES pilot schemes. From the account, it appears to have achieved its objective.

PROVIDING AN AGENDA FOR DISCUSSION BETWEEN PARENTS, STAFF AND STUDENTS

The report provides the basis for a structured discussion between parents and teachers. Some schools in the pilot study have also invited students[16] to join them while others have encouraged parents to use the report for constructive dialogue with their children at home. The dialogue provides the opportunity for staff to explain the recording procedures, and in so doing inevitably have to make reference to course objectives and content. Hence parents gain some insight into what each subject teacher aims to achieve yet in the context of their children, thus giving the discourse added relevance.

AIDING DIAGNOSIS OF STUDENTS' ACHIEVEMENTS

This objective arises from the preceding one in that the recording of achievement in terms of individual criteria enables strengths and weaknesses to be identified and new targets set. If students can be present on these occasions then all the better, for this would lend itself to a 'team' approach to learning in which all the members could share their hopes and anxieties. While the emphasis in this objective is diagnosis, it is clear that many parents view their children's achievements in a norm referenced way. They wish to know where they stand in relation to their peers, and also how teachers rate their chances in public examinations. It is difficult for staff to reconcile, in this context, two elements which are essentially different, that is, criterion and norm referencing. This is not just a difference in view between parents and teachers. Some staff are having difficulty in coming to terms with it.

At Brant for example, on a particular parents' evening, while the senior management had earlier explained the new recording arrangements, some colleagues were still using the marks in their record books as the agenda for discussion. When this anomaly was pointed out to the senior management, the explanation revealed an obstacle which could be fundamental to the introduction of records of achievement. They argued that the teachers were not using the criterion referenced approach to the discussion because they had not yet gained the confidence to do so. To achieve this, encouragement and support has got to be maintained, not only by the senior management and the LEA, but more specifically through close identification of inservice training (INSET) needs, which address the range of problems facing individual departments and referred to in Chapter 3.

However, despite these difficulties, parental support for records of achievement seems very strong, and is welcomed, not only in terms of the students' welfare, but is clearly a development which is fulfilling the schools' accountability to the community.

The role of management

In Chapters 2–4 frequent reference has been made to the role of senior management, and, as it is crucial to the development of records of achievement, it is important that it is considered as an entity in its own right. Experience at Brant and Winton as a whole would suggest that Broadfoot and Baines'[17] conclusion that three elements are vital to the successful introduction of records of achievement is totally accepted. These are commitment and leadership of the head and senior management team, the role of the coordinator and the involvement of as many staff as possible. This section will therefore be concerned with a discussion of these issues.

Commitment and leadership of senior management

Commitment to records of achievement assumes a complete understanding of the changes in philosophy that may be required. Some Winton headteachers and LEA staff, for example, view their introduction as being about the setting up of a new style recording system, as opposed to the internalisation of principles which place student ownership of learning and its implications as the priority. As was suggested in Chapter 2, Brant initially viewed records of achievement as a system but later came to tackle the philosophical issues. This was not by design so much as the pragmatic acknowledgement that a system provides tangible targets which can motivate both staff and students alike. It might be argued that the documentation provides the vehicle for changing the teacher–student relationship to one of a more balanced partnership for learning.

The point being made is that this is not always understood, and therefore an essential feature of commitment is a full understanding of the nature of an innovation which questions almost all aspects of school life. A successful move has already been made in this direction with NPRA TVEI Related Inservice Training (TRIST), but more initiatives require to be taken under Grant Related Inservice Training (GRIST) funding arrangements. The appointment of a development officer to promote and lead this work would be a worthwhile investment and an acknowledgement of its importance, which will take on added significance with the introduction of the assessment arrangements for the national curriculum.

Effective leadership stems from this appreciation, and any change which is as all embracing as the introduction of records of achievement requires the senior management to be closely identified with it. This was very apparent at Brant. The head, curriculum deputy and coordinators attended all the NPRA pilot school dissemination conferences, and were present at the inservice sessions and steering group meetings. The style of leadership attempted to achieve a balance between providing a sense of direction, without imposing a model of working, and allowing staff to develop their own ideas to enable them to learn from that experience. The aim was to encourage teacher ownership. The decision not to impose a common recording format for all departments (discussed in Chapter 3), but to support a variety of approaches, exemplifed this. However, it is perhaps symptomatic of their (and many other schools') lack of experience in this field that they could not anticipate the difficulties to be encountered by the subject specialists. As was pointed out in Chapter 3, there is a clear need for consultancy support in this area.

Teacher ownership is part of the corporate approach which the senior management has been keen to promote. In this respect the experience of the low attainers project, referred to earlier, was an important influence. The project was not seen to be 'owned' by the whole staff, because additional resources were provided for only a small part of the total curriculum. Similarly, group tutors have argued that a sense of corporate identity with records of achievement will not have been achieved until all year groups are involved. This view is based on the fact that what little additional resources the school has received have been devoted to the upper school, while staff, teaching mainly groups in years one to three, have been unable to get involved. This of course is an argument against the concept of a pilot scheme, but, bearing in mind the resource, staff development and coordination implications of introducing records to the whole school at any one time, it offers a pragmatic way forward. Another aspect of widening staff involvement has been the necessity to involve tutors more significantly in the management of records of achievement through increasing their representation on the school's steering group. This has been brought about as the importance of the group tutor role has been recognised. A more detailed discussion is found in Chapter 4.

The corporate ownership dimension was emphasised in Brant's plans to extend records of achievement to the remainder of the school. At a steering group meeting in June 1988 one of the coordinators put forward a suggestion that leadership of this development should involve less experienced staff in order that the initiative was not seen to be the preserve of a select few. This proposal (Figure 10) was not opposed and is in contrast with the observation in the PRAISE report (p 55) that 'The direct involvement of ordinary classroom teachers in the planning and conceptualisation of their projects has been rare.' With the obvious caveat that considerable staff development and management support will be required, the Brant strategy appears to have much to commend it as a means of widening expertise and stimulating interest in an innovation which is going to figure prominently in curriculum development for years to come.

RECORDS OF ACHIEVEMENT

A discussion document to explore the dissemination of good practices into the assessment and reporting systems of years 1 to 3

Development of good practice

The development of and the issuing of a fifth year Record of Achievement to all pupils has been proved possible. Although aspects of that development (both formative and summative) require some consolidation the systems used appear to work in this school. It is important that we now consider the principles and practices of Records of Achievement from a 'whole school' point of view. That is the extension of the principles and practices into the assessment and reporting processes of years 1 to 3.

Future validation by the NEA will probably require that the philosophy behind Records of Achievement apply to pupils 'throughout their time in compulsory education'.

This indicates a possible time scale of events:

1. All school leavers by 1995.
2. If validation is required for the 1995 leavers the principles and practices should be operating with the first year pupils in 1990.
3. A tentative step towards this would be to involve our first year intake due in September 1988.
4. Assessment and practices operating for an enhanced report July 1989.

The way forward

Aim: To develop an assessment and reporting style for years 1 to 3 that correlates with the processes in years 4 and 5.

These processes should include:

(a) Statements about what a pupil can do.
(b) Statements that describe skills and achievements.
(c) Assessments that actively involve the pupil (reviews – target setting – diagnosis).

(d) A rejection of the subjective comment after referring to personal and social characteristics rather than subject skills.

(e) The inclusion of the developments taking place in the third year.

Suggestions:

1. A move away from the limitations imposed by the cheque book style of report.
2. The development of a report that gives scope to report on subject criteria/skills/achievement.
3. A working party to examine how progress can be made. (An opportunity to involve staff who would like the experience of managing change).

Conclusion:

An enhanced style of report that involved the principles and practices currently used in the 4th and 5th year would move us cautiously into the 1990s and the demands that will then be made.

L Hunter
Coordinator

Figure 10 *Discussion document for the extension of records of achievement to years 1 to 3*

Coordination

The importance of the role of coordinator is widely accepted. PRAISE and the interim reports of both the NPRA and national pilot schemes all emphasise the need for it to be given adequate status, whether it is prescribed or acquired. In most schools a senior member of staff, sometimes the deputy head, takes responsibility, but in one Winton school a junior member of staff is in charge with the full support of the headteacher and staff. Here it has been recognised that knowledge, expertise and leadership traits are more important than formal status without these qualities. Furthermore, it is a step towards the corporate approach discussed above. However, decisions of this kind are comparatively rare, largely because the nature of records of achievement demands that coordinators have an overview of the curriculum, and usually it is only the senior management who are in this position.

The following appear to be emerging as key coordinator roles:

1. To lead, with other members of the senior management team, in the promotion of records of achievement by creating an awareness of their nature and implications for the curriculum.

2. To be sensitive to staff development needs and match them with the necessary INSET provision.
3. To promote corporate involvement in decision making.
4. To organise the logistics of records in particular, in relation to time, secretarial support, the formative to summative timetable (Figure 11) and the contributions of students and staff.
5. To be the link person through the headteacher between the school and the LEA with respect to resource needs and publicity.
6. To liaise closely with the national/local/regional scheme to which the school/LEA might be associated.
7. To be involved in dissemination either as a recipient or leader as part of accountability and as an aid to monitoring the school's practice.
8. To promote the value of records with users such as parents, employers and post-16 institutions.

Such wide-ranging responsibilities obviously require time and most coordinators are allocated some time for these duties. However, evidence from PRAISE (p 64) suggests that this is not just a 'start up' requisite but is necessary even when the project is off the ground. At Brant there are joint coordinators, which is not common. This has the advantage of enabling duties to be shared. One is primarily concerned with the logistics while the other leads the development aspect. The deputy head takes overall responsibility and in turn is answerable to the headteacher. The deputy's interest is strong and active, enhanced because he is also a member of the NPRA's Records of Achievement Committee, its key decision making body. While this shared concern is admirable, it is dependent upon the role definitions being made clear to all involved otherwise communication can be hindered. For example, one tutor was concerned that the line of communication was not facilitating decision making because responsibilities were not well defined.

The role of the LEA

Numerous references have been made in this and previous chapters regarding the role of the LEA. Resourcing and inservice training provision are the principal ones. Concerning resources, financial constraints will obviously play a part. A full appreciation of the nature of what is intended, which was referred to earlier as important in changing attitudes, is also crucial to acknowledging the level of funding necessary. In particular, the provision of additional staffing to allow for effective coordination and tutor/student discussions is a prime requi-

---

BRANT HIGH SCHOOL

RECORDS OF ACHIEVEMENT

TIMETABLE OF EVENTS – 5th YEAR

DATE	ACTIVITY
14 Sept.–24 Oct.	Issuing of verification slips (success in areas other than academic subjects) to pupils. Explanation will be made to the 5th year in Assembly.
2 Nov.	Verification lists/slips to be sent for typing.
14 Sept.–20 Nov.	Preparation through discussion with pupil draft ideas for testimonial (NPRA time).
14 Sept.–1 Oct.	Typing of curriculum profiles.
23 Nov.–11 Dec.	1. Mock Exams. 2. Subject profiles to be completed by 11 Dec. Collected/collated by Heads of Department and sent to coordinator.
14 Dec.–16 Jan. 1988	Typing/computer production of subject profiles.
25 Jan.–19 Feb.	Preparation of final testimonial by form tutors.
19 Feb.–11 March	Testimonials to typist.
14 March–18 March	Compilation of Record by Form Tutor/Year Tutor/Coordinator.
24 March	Record of Achievement issued.

IMPORTANT

It is hoped that by this date the NPRA will have validated our efforts.

NPRA validation will be inserted before issuing.

Figure 11 *Records of achievement timetable*

site. Inservice training has already been referred to in this context and LEAs have the opportunity through GRIST arrangements to make records of achievement a priority under the heading of assessment.

However, underpinning these areas must be a strong identification with the ideas fundamental to records of achievement. This will clearly signal to headteachers where priorities lie. This is sometimes done by implication rather than by obvious commitment. For example, at Winton the secondary headteachers[18] have asked the authority to give a clear lead; the response has been to point out that support for TVEI implies encouragement for records of achievement. (It was stated earlier that records of achievement are a mandatory part of TVEI, but also that it only provides for the 14–18 age range.) Leadership of a direct nature is what is required and the appointment of a curriculum adviser with responsibility for this field would be evidence that the Borough had acknowledged that there is an obligation to be met. Indeed, LEAs who have not done this already may have seriously to consider such an appointment in view of the Government's intention to implement the DES Statement of Policy in 1990 and the record of achievement implications of the national curriculum assessment arrangements.

Accreditation

The need for accreditation of records of achievement is another strand of accountability to the user, in that it aims to give reassurance as to the 'quality' of the summative document. Its rationale and possible mode of implementation is outlined in the DES Statement of Policy (para 33):

> If employers and others are to make use of the summary records, they will need as much assurance as possible about the accuracy, reliability and significance of the information given in them. The Secretaries of State believe that these needs may best be met by arrangements under which the systems which schools use for compiling and checking the summary record should be 'accredited' by an outside organisation such as a group of LEAs or an examining body or a consortium of LEAs and examining bodies.

The NPRA accepts this notion, but before implementation it was important to gain the experience of the pilot study from which criteria might be determined. However, as a step towards this objective it was agreed to validate the records of achievement of the pilot study schools in terms of the statements included on the first page of Brant's summative document (see pp 76–84 and Appendix 5). It will be noted that it is certified that Brant 'has adopted approaches consistent with NPRA guidelines'. These were included in Chapter 2 (Figure 3). It will be observed that the phrase 'should aim to' is significant in that it denotes that Brant is 'en route' towards the principles of good practice.

From the pilot study experience the NPRA is in the process (July 1988) of producing accreditation criteria. A draft document has suggested that they might include 15 elements which range over formative processes, the summative record and the management of the school. They cover the NPRA principles and many of those which were in the DES Statement of Policy, but some additions are of interest and support concerns expressed earlier in this book. Three are of particular note.

1. In Chapter 3 the question of negative statements was discussed. The draft criteria follow the line adopted at Brant; that is, the formative process may include the identification of weaknesses while the summative document must be wholly positive. This allows for the formative to take on its important diagnostic function of setting targets to promote students' strengths and remedy limitations.
2. The draft criteria suggest that 'common approaches to assessment are agreed between teachers'. The question of standardisation was raised in Chapter 3. While this may cause problems for subject departments, it is in line with the recommendation of the Task Group on Assessment and Testing (TGAT) Report[19] which asserts that there should be no less than four but no more than six criteria (called profile components in the Report).
3. Lastly, the DES Statement of Policy is concerned with secondary education although it does ask that primary experience should be taken into account. The draft criteria state that 'The centre (ie the school) will involve all students throughout their time in compulsory education in its procedures for recording achievement.' This would appear to be preparing for the time when records of achievement are introduced formally into primary education. If so, a host of other issues are raised about the validity of such criteria as student ownership and reviewing in terms of student maturity, the place of the summative document(s) and what information should be included. In Chapter 6 these matters will be discussed further in the context of the implementation of the TGAT report.

It must be remembered that the criteria are at present in draft form and may be altered, but their scope suggests that they match the all embracing nature of records of achievement. This in turn raises the question of implementation, the form it should take and who would undertake it. In Chapter 1 it was suggested that a task of this nature and magnitude would require a comprehensive appraisal of almost all aspects of school life, not unlike the range of an HMI full inspection. If this is the case, what models of operation should be considered? At national level no paradigm has yet been put forward, although one is anticipated when the national steering committee produces its final report on the pilot schemes in the latter part of 1988. However, its interim report (p 12) does make the point that 'at this juncture we do not expect to propose arrangements which necessarily require involvement beyond the local authority'. If this assertion becomes a firm recommendation, the value of such consortia as the NPRA, EMRAP, OCEA and others will be lost.

The notion of partnership between LEAs and examination boards has been much valued in the NPRA as can be witnessed in its growth from fewer than 10 LEAs to 37 over a period of less than four years and the popularity of its unit accreditation and record of achievement schemes. One of the main attractions to LEAs joining has been the opportunity for students to be given credit by an examining body for achievements and experiences not normally covered by public examinations. If LEAs are going to have to take sole responsibility for accreditation, the credibility of their records may be questioned. This may be on the grounds of expertise available, particularly in small LEAs such as Winton, or it might be that delegation would lead to such a wide variety of records that it would only add to the problem of gaining their acceptance with users. Furthermore, a development of this kind would not assist employment mobility even within a metropolitan area. For example, in Greater Manchester nine records of achievement would be available and, while it may be argued that they would all be following national guidelines, there is inevitably going to be different interpretations and practices, which may lead to differing degrees of credibility.

With regard to the accreditation process itself, most of the national schemes, like the NPRA, are at the stage of developing pilot frameworks. The East Midland Record of Achievement Project (EMRAP) is piloting a six-stage process[20] which will stretch over a period of three to five years before a school is likely to be considered for full accreditation status. A brief summary of the stages is as follows:

1. A school reviews its practice in relation to the commitments, implicit and explicit, in accepting the principles of EMRAP and, as a result, decides to apply for registration.

2. Dialogue then takes place between the school and at least three local people with a minimum composition of an LEA officer, a local consortium representative and a practitioner (a fellow professional of the school's choosing). The intention here is to ensure that there are no fundamental contradictions between school practice and EMRAP principles. If there are, they will be referred back for clarification of intentions and to assist in the identification of development needs.
3. The school would then make a presentation to the EMRAP Accreditation Group showing how its practice is moving towards embracing the EMRAP principles. This will lead to agreeing targets for development by the school. The Accreditation Group will then decide whether to accredit the school with either *Registered Status* or *Full Status*. The former will indicate that the school has satisfied basic requirements and has a clear development plan, while the latter denotes that the school has in place practices which fully involve pupils in processes embodying the EMRAP principles.
4. The development stage provides for discussion between the Accreditation Group and the school to establish inservice training arrangements to help meet the targets identified in stage 3.
5. The school now implements the development programme agreed at stage 3.
6. Finally, there is a review stage which is likely to take place after a three-year period. The school's progress towards the target is reviewed and new ones set.

This format appears to have the advantage of being diagnostic, supportive and encouraging. Responsibility for joining the scheme is firmly placed upon individual schools thus ensuring that they are likely to be favourably disposed towards EMRAP principles. These factors together with the voluntary nature of the scheme suggest that very few schools will not eventually obtain full status. However, if the proposed national guidelines (to be put forward in the final report of the Records of Achievement National Steering Committee (RANSC)) argue for a mandatory as opposed to a voluntary system, accreditation could be divisive in that some schools, for circumstances beyond their control, may never meet the criteria and so might appear 'second class' in the eyes of students and other users.

The credibility of accreditation will of course not only relate to the status of the accrediting body but depend on the rigour and thoroughness of the process. It may be that national guidelines might suggest an accreditation period, at the end of which schools would have to undergo a review in order to keep their status. Alternatively, schools which do not meet criteria entirely could be given a limited period accreditation supervised by the LEA before full status is given.

In British Columbia (BC) courses in secondary schools are accredited by the State on this kind of basis. Briefly, a school spends a year undertaking a curriculum review which it documents in the form of an Accreditation Book. This is laid before an accreditation team drawn from the State office and school boards (the BC equivalent to LEAs). It is composed of high school principals, school board and State officials. The team spends a week in the school discussing the review and looking at practice, at the end of which the courses are accredited for a given time. The maximum period is six years, and anything less than five is not considered acceptable. This usually means strong action by the school board to remedy the situation, and could include the redeployment of senior staff.

In an extreme case where accreditation for only one or two years was given, the State could withdraw the school's responsibility to award up to 50 per cent of the marks in BC's school-leaving examination and institute its own assessment procedures. The remaining 50 per cent is assessed by external examinations conducted by the State. Whether a system of this sort has anything to offer the accreditation of records of achievement is of course open to debate. However, what is certain is that a rolling programme of accreditation and review, which commands the respect of schools and users alike, will be essential.

Summary

1. The problems facing the tutor in the transition from formative recording into the summative document are discussed.

2. The question of brevity in relation to users' requirements is considered, and it is argued that they may be difficult to reconcile with the principle of student ownership.

3. The verification of achievements is considered and the problem of their 'shelf life' touched upon.

4. Dissatisfaction with the limitations of the computer in producing subject reports is outlined.

5. The need for context is discussed in relation to users' needs.

6. The presentation of the students' contribution and their use of the

summative document are considered. Concerning the latter, training is thought to be a necessity.

7. The composition of the summative document is reviewed in terms of the place of negative comments, objectivity, consistency and standardisation.

8. Concern is expressed at indications which suggest that records of achievement have not been positively accepted in post-16 institutions.

9. The positive and valued response of parents is recognised but some potential pitfalls of language and communication are identified along with examples of how they might be overcome.

10. The commitment and leadership of senior management is looked at in terms of the nature of records of achievement, teacher 'ownership', corporate development and the roles of the coordinator(s).

11. The importance of LEA resourcing informed by a thorough understanding of the nature of records is argued. Close identification with the values underpinning them would give a much appreciated lead to the schools.

12. The question of accreditation is discussed in relation to draft criteria, process and timescale. The EMRAP pilot scheme and course accreditation in British Columbia are used to illustrate possible ways forward.

References

1. MCCI (1987) *An Employer's View of Records of Achievement* A paper from the Records of Achievement Working Party, para 15.
2. Op cit, para 10.
3. *Interim Report* Spring 1988.
4. The Industrial Society (1987) *The Achievements of Robert Arthur, Essex.*
5. DES Welsh Office (1987) *Records of Achievement: An Interim Report.*
6. Burgess, T and Adams, E (1985) *Records of Achievement at 16.* NFER, Nelson.
7. This statement is made in the context of the national pilot schemes and referred to in the PRAISE report, p 41.
8. See Reference 4, p 2.
9. *Records of Achievement – The CBI View* (1983).
10. That is, the MICC, Essex and Wigan Groups.
11. See Reference 5.

12. See Appendix 1 to Reference 4 (above).
13. See for example the Wigan Employers Liaison Sub-Group, Reference 3.
14. See for example St Peters RC Comprehensive School, Orrell, Wigan.
15. East Midlands Record of Achievement Project, Newsletter 4, Spring 1988.
16. See for example the Nugent RC High School, Liverpool.
17. Broadfoot, P and Baines, B (1987) *Interim External Evaluation Report, Pilot Study in the Accreditation of Centres for Records of Achievement 1986–88.*
18. This was requested in a discussion paper on the management implications of records of achievement produced by Winton TVEI, January 1988.
19. DES and Welsh Office (1988) *National Curriculum Task Group Assessment and Testing Report. A Digest for Schools* p 21.
20. Summarised from the EMRAP Report to RANSC, Appendix IV.

Chapter 6

Records of Achievement and the National Curriculum

This chapter is concerned with prospects for the future development of records. In particular, the main issue to be considered will be their place in the context of the introduction of the assessment arrangements for the national curriculum. Reference has already been made to the work of the Task Group on Assessment and Testing (TGAT), and it is these proposals which will provide the focus for discussion. The Government[1] has decided, in light of responses to them, to adopt the following principles as the basis for a national system of assessment and testing related to the national curriculum attainment targets:

1. Attainment targets will be set which establish what children should normally be expected to know, understand and be able to do at the ages of 7, 11, 14 and 16; these will enable the progress of each child to be measured against national standards.
2. Pupils' performance in relation to attainment targets should be assessed and reported on at ages 7, 11, 14 and 16. Attainment targets should be grouped for this purpose to make the assessment and reporting manageable.
3. Different levels of attainment and overall pupil progress demonstrated by tests and assessment should be registered on a 10-point scale covering all the years of compulsory schooling.
4. Assessment should be by a combination of national external tests and assessment by teachers. At the age of 16 the GCSE will be the main form of assessment, especially in the core subjects of English, mathematics and science.
5. The results of tests and other assessments should be used both formatively to help better teaching and to inform decisions about next steps for a pupil, and summatively at ages 7, 11, 14 and 16 to inform parents about their child's progress.
6. Detailed results of assessments of individual pupils should be given

in full to parents, and the Government attaches great importance to the principle that these reports should be simple and clear. Individual results should not be published, but aggregated results at the ages of 11, 14 and 16 should be so that the wider public can make informed judgements about attainment in a school or LEA. There should be no legal requirement for schools to publish such results for seven-year-olds, though it is strongly recommended that schools should do so.

7. In order to safeguard standards, assessments made by teachers should be compared with the results of the national tests and with the judgement of other teachers.

Standardisation and teacher ownership

With regard to the first principle, the imposition of the attainment targets[2] which will be identified by the core subject groups of mathematics, English and science, and the foundation subjects of geography, history, technology, art, music, physical education plus a modern language (for students of secondary school age only) is a further development of the need for standardisation recognised in Chapters 3 and 5. However, it was also argued that an important element in managing records of achievement at Brant had been to encourage teacher ownership as a necessary aspect of corporate development. If teachers do not 'own' the attainment targets, this may hinder their introduction. Experience of developing records of achievement has shown that, where teachers feel they have had a major involvement in the innovation, it is likely to take root. It would seem that no attempt has been made to reconcile the needs of wide teacher participation and the standardisation of assessment criteria and procedures.

Pre-specified objectives

It is also worth re-stating here the point made in Chapter 3 with regard to prescribed objectives. Attainment targets do not take into account those subject areas where the emphasis is upon giving the student an experience, the learning outcome of which is not pre-specified. Aspects of the creative arts come into this category.

Attainment targets and personal attributes

Also in Chapter 3 the problems facing departments with regard to the potentially difficult area of recording personal traits were discussed. In particular, it was suggested that attainment targets might command priority consideration. There is no reason to believe that this will not be the case. The TGAT report makes it clear (p 7) that it is not concerned with the assessment of attitudes, and the national curriculum is to receive such high priority, as far as the Government is concerned, that it will not be surprising if subject teachers do not feel encouraged to give a rounded picture of their student. If this is the case then it will only promote further the notion of the 'pastoral–academic divide', and the recording of personal attributes could become the preserve of group tutors. This would be a backward step, particularly as in subjects such as mathematics and English teachers are likely to have more contact time with students than the respective pastoral staff. Furthermore, if the idea of records of achievement presenting a rounded picture of students' achievement and experience is not to become redundant, it is imperative that these are viewed in a wide range of contexts in order that the portrayal has validity.

Student ownership and participation

Concerning the second principle on p 109 – pupils' performance in relation to attainment targets – this again calls into question the issue of student ownership. If achievement is to be reported on at the ages of 7, 11, 14 and 16, these will in effect become summative or interim summative records. It has not been the aim of this book to consider records of achievement in terms of the primary age range where the concept of ownership raises different questions, but with reference to 14- and 16-year-olds, as was discussed in Chapters 4 and 5, its importance is central. It is linked to the difficult area of negative recording in this instance. It will be remembered that the DES Statement of Policy asserts that the summative document should be a positive statement of achievement. The national curriculum reporting arrangements will include data which will indicate where students have failed to reach national standard, and low attaining students are likely to have little respect for a record which lists their limitations. Ownership also includes the right to determine its composition and to whom it should be shown, but as reporting to parents will be mandatory (see principles 5 and 6 on p 109), this prerogative will be redundant.

With reference to the general idea of student involvement, principle 5 concerning the use of test and assessment results is supportive at the formative stage. While this is to be applauded as a diagnostic approach towards better informed teaching, the problems facing even the best intentioned departments in this area (see Chapter 3) must be listened to sympathetically and taken on board. There are likely to be resource implications here if this principle is to be implemented.

The specification of profile components and achievement levels

The core and foundation subject groups have been asked to identify 10 levels of attainment (principle 3 on p 109) across the age range 5–16. To achieve these, the groups have to divide their subjects into four, not more than six profile components. The components (which will consist of the clustered attainment targets mentioned above and exemplified in Reference 2) will be assessed separately to give a profile, and the scores will then be aggregated to obtain a subject result at each of the ten levels. This exercise is very similar to that discussed in Chapter 1 in relation to grade-related criteria when subjects were split into domains (now called profile components) and three levels identified. The problems encountered then in terms of number of domains, unity of the subject level definition, etc were considerable. To undertake such a task, therefore, over 10 levels and the 5–16 age range is daunting. It is not surprising that the TGAT second supplementary report (1988) advises 'that initially it may be necessary to adopt a somewhat rough and ready approach to the establishment of profile components and levels of progression, for the sake of getting the system up and running'. If what is to be imposed is 'rough and ready', it will not encourage confidence in a national assessment system, and will almost inevitably have a 'knock on' effect in the schools as teachers attempt to assess students' performance against criteria which will perhaps fall short of being totally workable.

Cross-curricular components

An aspect of the task facing the subject working groups, which perhaps underlines the problems of implementation, is the request from the TGAT report that

> Wherever possible, one or more components should have more general application across the curriculum; for these a single common specification should be adopted in each of the subjects concerned. (para 35)

The cross-curricular implications of this are spelt out further in the second TGAT supplementary report which explains

> ... where aspects of a profile component seem likely to be common to two or more subjects, a co-ordinating mechanism of some kind will be needed to decide which subjects they should be allocated, or how they could or should be shared between the subjects while avoiding unnecessary duplication. Here we suggest that the working group for English should be asked to consider which components, relating to written and oral communication skills, should be regarded as common to some or all other identified subjects, as well as those which would be appropriate only to English as such. (p 20)

Presumably mathematics would take a similar lead regarding number and so on.

The *coordinating mechanism of some kind* suggestion may be worked out at the level of the subject working group in terms of criteria although, as was discussed in Chapter 3, there are difficulties to be overcome. However, when it comes to the assessment procedures in schools the implications are far-reaching, in organisational arrangements alone. To speculate on how this might operate is of interest. In the English example quoted above it could be decided that written and oral communication is common to all the core and foundation subjects. An English department implementing principles 1 to 5 mentioned on pp 109–110, with respect to assessing and reporting on students at the age of 14, would have to organise the assessment of these skills taking into account that they will be performed in a variety of contexts and therefore have different connotations. This would be taking place at an age when students' attainments are anticipated to span four of the 10 achievement levels (Figure 12).

Of course, 'easier' approaches may be found but the magnitude of the task when multiplied by the many cross-curricular areas is formidable. In Chapter 3 it was argued that recording achievement in this area required national priority before it could be effected. The TGAT report attempts to give it that status. If the Government intends to implement fully its recommendations then it will have to accept the resource implication (particularly time) which the above outline example suggests will be a basic requirement.

Parental involvement, GCSE and socio-economic factors

The TGAT proposal to assess the profile components separately will provide the data for student–teacher discussion and opportunities for self assessment at the formative stage, and also the agenda for structured consideration with parents. In Chapter 5 it was argued that parents welcome more informative school reports. Principle 6 on p 109

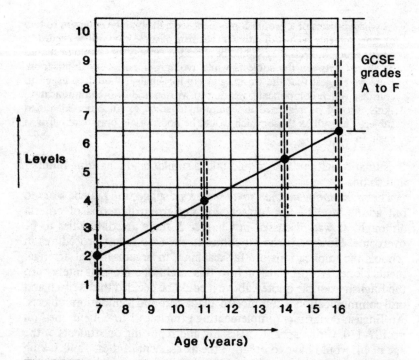

The GCSE grades A–F have been added to show their relationship with achievement levels.

The sloping line represents the average educational progress of children over about two years.

The vertical broken lines show the expected range of student attainment at the ages of reporting. It will be seen that at the age of 14 some students will have achieved levels equal to GCSE grades.

Figure 12 *Sequence of pupil achievement of levels between ages 7 and 16 taken from the National Curriculum Task Group on Assessment and Testing Report: a digest for schools (p 9)*

– which concerns what should be done with the results of pupils' assessments – fully endorses this view. However, at the reporting ages it will be mandatory to inform them where their children stand both within the school and nationally. Some parents will welcome this while others will prefer a wholly positive document in line with the DES Statement of Policy, particularly if their child is not a high achiever. It will not encourage parents to be active partners in the education service if all they receive are results which list their children's limitations.

Two other issues arise in the context of the reporting of results. One, their relationship with GCSE, and secondly, the socio-economic circumstances in which they are achieved. With regard to one, principle 4 on p 109 affirms that GCSE will be the main form of assessment. The TGAT Report (para 105) asserts that the boundary between levels six and seven should correspond to the F/G grade boundary for GCSE, although the first supplementary report (p 9) states that this will not necessarily be the case in all subjects.

Despite the caveat, this relationship between levels and grades might suggest to some parents and other users that a GCSE should be awarded when this standard is achieved. For example, Figure 12 indicates that it is anticipated at the age of 14 that a substantial minority of students will have achieved grade F and higher. If this is to be the case, then principle 4 – on assessment as a combination of national external tests and assessment by teachers – will be undermined in some foundation subjects and, despite the insistence that GCSE will be the main form of assessment in mathematics, English and science, its status may well be queried with the introduction of achievement levels. Bearing in mind the discussion in Chapter 5 regarding the problem of communicating the aims of records of achievement to employers, explaining the complexity of achievement levels and how they are arrived at is a formidable task. It is gratifying to note that a pilot study is proposed with this objective in mind.

In relation to the socio-economic circumstances in which a school's results at the reporting ages are achieved, the TGAT Report argues that this is best done by the LEA producing a statement by way of explanation to accompany the report. In Chapter 4, the problem of disadvantage in terms of students' opportunities to record achievements was considered and the sensitivities of such situations acknowledged. In placing this broader responsibility upon the LEAs, TGAT accepts the difficulties. It admits:

> Such statements will obviously need sensitive preparation and, as they should include information on the extent of the influence of background factors on performance, local authorities will need technical advice in their preparation.

It remains to be seen how many LEAs will find this acceptable with the likelihood of 'labelling' being an obvious concern, as well as the funding of such an exercise.

Curriculum review

In this book the use of records of achievement as a starting point for curriculum review has been referred to as and when it appeared appropriate, such as their impact on teaching style, the identification of assessment criteria, etc. Some NPRA schools have used the introduction of records with this a central aim. They embarked upon the exercise from the standpoint of student needs. The TGAT first supplementary report (p 13) infers that review will be assessment led. It states:

> A special factor in this context (of review) is that curriculum specifications often need to be reconsidered in the light of assessment experience.

If student needs are not the starting point, then there is the danger that assessment, rather than being the servant of the curriculum will be dictating it. Schools may be inhibited in considering change if they know that potential outcomes are going to be governed by the assessment instruments.

Conclusion

To conclude, while the TGAT report recommends 'the use of Records of Achievement as a vehicle for recording progress and achievement within the national assessment system' (para 162), it has been suggested above that there are tensions between the two. It will be noted that the national curriculum has brought the relationship between the three dimensions to records of achievement identified in Chapter 1 – that is, student needs, subject reporting and accountability – into sharp focus. The need for accountability underpins the other two but now the emphasis is clearly focused on subject reporting with a view to the achievement of national standards. On the other hand, a strong feature of the records of achievement 'movement' has been its student orientation, hence the value placed on ownership and recognition of positive accomplishment. In terms of the national curriculum, it seems inevitable that the students' role will be limited to the formative stage and the extra-curricular aspects of the summative record.

The Government's strategy is to identify attainment targets and assess their achievement by external tests and teacher assessment. It remains to be seen whether this will have the desired effect. Initial indications from experience of records of achievement at Brant suggest that another route to raising standards is by making students feel they are valued as a means of gaining their cooperation to achieve this end. The challenge to the teaching profession will, therefore, be to ensure that the values which focus upon the needs of individual students are not forfeited to the cause of national standards. It is for the future good of the education service that the two must be reconciled.

Summary

1. The principles upon which the Government intend to base the assessment of the national curriculum are spelt out.

2. It was argued that there was a need to reconcile the need for teacher ownership with the imposition of criteria.

3. The point was re-stated that pre-specified objectives do not take into account certain curricular needs.

4. The question of student ownership and participation was discussed. While the TGAT proposals aimed to promote participation at the formative stage, the concept of ownership with its attendant emphasis on positive recording appears to be threatened.

5. Bearing in mind the difficulties encountered in the Grade Related Criteria exercise considered in Chapter 1, it is suggested that the core and foundation subject groups will be facing formidable problems, and the introduction of 'rough and ready' criteria was not likely to encourage confidence in a national assessment system.

6. The TGAT recommendation for the assessment of profile components was looked at in terms of the organisational implications, and a speculative example was given of the difficulties likely to be encountered.

7. The individual assessment of the profile components provide the basis for an agenda for teacher–parent discussion at the formative stage, but concern was expressed regarding the dissemination of results at the reporting ages when they were no more than a catalogue of students' limitations.

8. The relationship between achievement levels and GCSE grades was examined and the suggestion made that the former could undermine the status of the latter.

9. It was suggested that there were difficulties in using socio–economic factors to explain student performance.

10. It was argued that assessment led curriculum review could restrict consideration of outcomes to those which could be easily assessed.

11. Lastly, it was pointed out that the relationship between records of achievement and the national curriculum assessment procedures was an uneasy one, and that the challenge for the teaching profession was to defend and promote the values underpinning records while at the same time accommodating the new demands.

References

1. Announcement by the Secretary of State for Education and Science, Mr Kenneth Baker, in answer to a question from Mr Robert Key MP, 7 June 1988.
2. An example of an attainment target is 'the ability to assign an organism to its major group on the basis of observable features'. This is taken from 'Living things and their interaction with the environment' – a theme identified by the Interim Report of the National Curriculum Science Group. A more detailed definition of attainment targets than is in the text is included in the DES Welsh Office publication *The National Curriculum 5–16*, a consultative document, July 1987.

Selected Recommended Reading

Important preliminary reading

DES Welsh Office (1984) *Records of Achievement: A Statement of Policy.*
DES Welsh Office (1987) *Records of Achievement: An Interim Report.*
DES and Welsh Office (1988) *National Curriculum Mathematics Working Group – Final Report.*
DES and Welsh Office (1988) *National Curriculum Science Working Group – Final Report.*
DES and Welsh Office (1988) *National Curriculum Task Group on Assessment and Testing.*
DES and Welsh Office (1988) *National Curriculum Task Group on Assessment and Testing Report – A Digest for Schools.*
DES and Welsh Office (1988) *Records of Achievement – Final Report.*
Hitchcock, Gloria (1986) *Profiles and Profiling: A practical introduction.* Longman.
HMSO (1987) *The National Curriculum 5–16*, a consultative document.
The Industrial Society/Essex County Council (1987) *The Achievements of Robert Arthur, Essex* The Industrial Society.
Interim Evaluation Report (1987) *Pilot Records of Achievement in Schools Evaluation (PRAISE)* Open University/Bristol University.
Law Bill (1984) *Uses and Abuses of Profiling* Harper Education.

Useful background texts

Black, H and Broadfoot, P (1982) *Keeping Track of Teaching* Routledge & Kegan Paul.
Broadfoot, P (1987) *Introducing Profiling: A Practical Manual* Macmillan.
Burgess, T and Adams, E (1980) *Outcomes of Education* Macmillan.
Burgess, T and Adams, E (1985) *Records of Achievement at 16* NFER-Nelson.

Reference material

County Hall, Dorchester (1987) *National Profiling Network*.

Garforth, D and Macintosh, H G (1986) *Profiling: A Users' Manual* Stanley Thornes.

NPRA Pilot Study in the Accreditation of Centres for Records of Achievement 1986–88 Booklet for Centres and LEAs. March 1986.

Records of Achievement Resource Pack. SCDC, Newcombe House, 45 Notting Hill Gate, London W11 3JB.

Early developments

Balogh, J (1982) *Profile Reports for School Leavers* Schools Council. Longman Resources Unit.

Further Education Unit (1984) *Profiles in Action*.

Goacher, B (1983) *Schools Council Programme 5, Recording Achievement at 16+* Longman.

SCRE (1977) *Part 1, Pupils in Profile* Hodder & Stoughton.

Appendix 1

Appendices A and B of the SEC Draft Criteria Geography Report

APPENDIX A: Level two criteria: Preliminary statement

The Working Party considers that the criteria for level two in each domain should be seen as an extension of level one and that criteria such as the following would be indicative of this level. These criteria are given as examples and in no way constitute a complete list of level two criteria in Geography.

A SPECIFIC GEOGRAPHICAL KNOWLEDGE

 In relation to areas and topics implied by a particular GCSE syllabus, the candidate has demonstrated the ability to:

 (i) recall a range of factual material given considerable guidance.

B GEOGRAPHICAL UNDERSTANDING

 In relation to spatial and environmental patterns, processes and relationships at a variety of scales, the candidate has demonstrated the ability to:

 (i) offer simple explanations;
 (ii) describe associations between not more than three sets of information.

C MAP AND GRAPHIC SKILLS

 In relation to the use and production of maps, graphs, diagrams and pictorial material, the candidate has demonstrated the ability to:

 (i) extract a wide range of specified information, using reference systems, conventional signs and scales, given detailed instructions;
 (ii) construct simple graphs, given data and axes (only).

D APPLICATION OF GEOGRAPHY TO ECONOMIC, ENVIRONMENTAL, POLITICAL AND SOCIAL ISSUES

 In relation to examples, by applying geographical understanding and skills, the candidate has demonstrated the ability to:

 (i) recognise and describe an issue arising from the use of resources or space;
 (ii) identify a range of problems arising from conflicting demands on resources and space.

E GEOGRAPHICAL ENQUIRY

In relation to structured enquiry, given specific guidance by the teacher at key stages, the candidate has demonstrated the ability to achieve the objectives specified at level one and to undertake some extension of this work as a result of personal initiative.

APPENDIX B

DOMAIN DEFINITIONS

PROPOSED CRITERIA

Level 1

A. Specific geographical knowledge

This domain refers to the ability to locate selected places accurately and to recall basic factual information.
In relation to areas and topics implied by a particular GCSE syllabus, the candidate has demonstrated the ability to:

(i) identify located principal features;
(ii) recall factual material given a structured task;
(iii) match terms with descriptions of processes or features;

B. Geographical understanding

This domain refers to the ability to offer explanations for spatial and environmental patterns, processes and relationships.
In relation to spatial and environmental patterns, processes and relationships at a variety of scales, the candidate has demonstrated the ability to:

(i) identify simple distributions and patterns;
(ii) describe associations between two sets of information;
(iii) identify temporal changes;

C. Map and graphic skills

This domain refers to the ability to extract and use geographical information from maps, graphs, diagrams and pictorial material and to communicate information using maps, graphs, diagrams and pictorial material.
In relation to the use and production of maps, graphs, diagrams and pictorial material, the candidate has demonstrated the ability to:

(i) use a co-ordinate reference system to locate places;
(ii) give the direction of one place from another;
(iii) translate the scale of an item into real terms;
(iv) use the key to identify features on maps;
(v) identify specified elements of the land-scape on maps and pictorial material;
(vi) extract specified geographical information from simple graphs and diagrams;
(vii) plan and describe or plan and follow a simple route.
(viii) plot data on graphs when axes and scales are provided;
(ix) add specified detail to partially completed material, including sketch-maps, using information provided;

D. Application of Geography to economic, environmental, political and social issues

This domain refers to the ability to apply geographical ideas and skills to an inter-pretation of the issues associated with social and economic patterns, the use of resources and the management of the environment.
In relation to examples, by applying geographical understanding and skills, the candidate has demonstrated the ability to:

(i) identify an issue arising from the use of resources or space;
(ii) appreciate the different attitudes to the issue that groups or individuals may hold;
(iii) identify one of the problems arising from conflicting demands on resources and space;
(iv) select or suggest a feasible resolution of the issue;

E. Geographical enquiry

This domain refers to the ability to parti-cipate in geographical investigations which include the identification of a question, the basic skills of data collection, seeking answers and explanations and presenting findings.

In relation to structured enquiry, given specific guidance by the teacher at all stages, the candidate has demonstrated the ability to:

(i) collect and record data from primary sources on provided recording materials by following precise instructions and using familiar procedures;
(ii) select relevant information under given headings from a limited number of secondary sources;
(iii) present the collected data in appropriate forms given step-by-step instructions;
(iv) present a commentary expressed basically in descriptive terms;
(v) comment on the application and usefulness of the findings.

122

FOR GCSE GEOGRAPHY

Level 3	Level 4

(i) identify and locate principal features;
(ii) recall a range of factual material given limited guidance;
(iii) provide definitions of technical terms used in Geography;
(iv) provide a basic description of geographical features and processes;

(i) identify and locate a combination of related features;
(ii) recall a range of factual material;
(iii) provide a comprehensive description or definition of geographical features and processes using appropriate terminology

(i) identify and explain the main characteristics of given distributions and patterns;
(ii) describe, and offer explanations for, the associations between information;
(iii) identify and explain temporal changes in human and physical landscapes.

(i) explain the significance of the regularities and associations identified within given distributions and patterns;
(ii) use ideas to analyse ways in which human and physical landscapes have evolved and predict how they may continue to evolve;
(iii) draw and justify inferences from data and arrive at reasoned explanations;
(iv) recognise that explanations are often incomplete and that there may be different interpretations of the same evidence.

(i) identify and describe the significant features of the human and physical landscape on maps;
(ii) extract information from the map appropriate to a specified topic;
(iii) use a map for a practical purpose;
(iv) describe variations and identify trends in information from two-dimensional graphs provided;
(v) propose an appropriate form of graphical representation for data provided;
(vi) describe landscapes or geographical phenomena from pictorial material;
(vii) translate information in diagram or sketch form into verbal statements;
(viii) prepare an annotated sketch in the field or from a photograph.

(i) draw inferences about the human and physical landscape by interpretation of map evidence;
(ii) use information from several sources to interpret a landscape;
(iii) identify and describe trends in information from more complex graphs provided;
(iv) communicate geographical information using an appropriate selection of maps, graphs, diagrams or pictorial forms.

(i) understand an issue that may arise from conflicting demands on resources and space;
(ii) appreciate that the different attitudes of groups and individuals to an issue reflect differing values, experiences and priorities;
(iii) explain how a variety of problems may arise from conflicting demands on resources and space;
(iv) suggest and justify a feasible resolution of an issue;

(i) understand that an issue arising from conflicting demands on resources and space may be complex;
(ii) analyse ways in which the values, experiences and priorities of groups and individuals may affect their attitudes to an issue;
(iii) explain how the definition of, and response to, a problem associated with the use of resources and space may be influenced by the values and attitudes of decision-makers;
(iv) suggest, analyse and comment upon different ways of resolving the issue.

Given general guidance on the structuring of enquiries and tutoring at key stages, the candidate has demonstrated the ability to:

(i) make geographically appropriate decisions about a suitable topic for enquiry, sources of information, strategies for data collection, forms of analysis and cartographic and symbolic means of presenting findings;
(ii) develop and use a range of practical skills, techniques or equipment to collect and process data from primary and secondary sources;
(iii) analyse the collected data and draw conclusions;
(iv) comment on the application and usefulness of findings and how the study could be extended;
(v) communicate the outcomes of the enquiry appropriately and clearly.

Given general guidance on structuring enquiries and occasional tutoring when sought, the candidate has demonstrated the ability to:

(i) show initiative and imagination in selecting a topic suitable for enquiry;
(ii) make decisions about geographically appropriate sources of information, strategies for data collection, forms of analysis and cartographic and symbolic means of presenting findings;
(iii) develop and use a range of practical skills, techniques or equipment to collect and process data from primary and secondary sources;
(iv) analyse the collected data and draw conclusions and possible implications;
(v) reflect and comment on the effectiveness of the enquiry, its findings, and possible application and extension;
(vi) communicate the outcomes of the enquiry appropriately and clearly.

123

Appendix 2

Extract from Frodsham High School Coordinated Science Guide Year 3 (1987/8) – pp 4–22 incl

4 Skills and Processes to be Learned and Assessed.

During the course you will improve your performance in the following skills and processes. We will assess your performance throughout the course.

1a) You will improve your <u>knowledge</u> of science.
 b) You will improve your <u>understanding</u> of science.
 c) You will learn to <u>use</u> your scientific knowledge.

2 You will learn to use apparatus and measuring instruments.

3 You will learn to <u>observe</u> carefully and record your observations accurately.

4 You will learn to plan and design experiments.

5 You will improve your communication skills, both spoken and non-spoken.

6 You will learn how to explore and investigate areas which are new to you by,
 i) practical investigations and,
 ii) data search using books, computers etc.

7 You will learn to work well with others.

8 You will see the importance of science in society by looking at some issues that are relevant to your life today.

How you are assessed.

5

First, the good news. There are no 'end of year exams' in science! However, there are several new ways of assessing your achievement. We hope that you will enjoy many of these assessments and learn to see them as a way of <u>improving your performance</u>.

CAN-DO TESTS.

These are simple tests to see if you can perform a stated task. For example, if you show your teacher that you <u>can</u> heat a substance safely, you will pass 'Can-Do Test No 16'. It's as simple as that ! A list of the Can-Do Tests used at present is given later.

SCIENCE SKILLS

Your teachers will decide the level at which you perform certain science skills. In order to help them be absolutely fair to you, they will measure how well you perform against a 'check-list'.

For example, suppose your teacher has decided to check how well you are carrying out the skill of OBSERVING. First of all, you will be given an experiment that is thought to be especially suitable to test this skill. Whilst you are carrying out the experiment, during the course of the lesson, your teacher will compare how you perform with the check list for the OBSERVING skill (See page 15). If you are noted 'taking a reading accurately', then you gain skill F1. If you are noted 'making particularly accurate observations', then you gain skill S11.

The skills can be passed at one of three levels :-

FOUNDATION, MERIT and SPECIAL.

To pass at Foundation Level it is necessary to gain any one of the Foundation Statements 1 - 5.
To pass at Merit Level it is necessary to gain any one of the Merit Statements 6 - 10.
To pass at the Special Level, it is necessary to gain any one of the Special Statements 11 - 15.

6

UNIT TESTS

These take place at the end of each unit. The tests can be taken at 3 separate levels :-

FOUNDATION, MERIT or SPECIAL.

Your teacher will help you decide which level of test to take. In order to pass a test, you need to score 18 out of 25 marks. If you score 17 marks then you will automatically be awarded the level below.

For example :-

Fred decides to take the 'Special Level' test in 'Gases'. He scores 19 and gains the Special level pass.
Well done Fred !

Sid also decides to take the Special Level test and scores 17. He goes down to the Merit level pass.
Not bad, Sid !

Tom takes the same paper and scores 15.
Sorry, Tom !

Tom and his teacher will now enter Tom for the paper at the Merit level. He'll be able to take the test in a special lunchtime session.
Good Luck, Tom !

WHICH TESTS ARE THE MOST IMPORTANT ?

7

In your new science course, the Can-Do tests and Science Skills count for about 70% of your final grade. They are therefore very important. The Unit tests count for the remaining 30%.

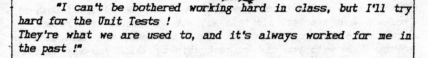

Jill says ....

"I can't be bothered working hard in class, but I'll try hard for the Unit Tests !
They're what we are used to, and it's always worked for me in the past !"

- Sorry Jill ! You may get good test marks, but they count for <u>less than one third</u> of your final assessment. And, in order to gain a high grade you must do well in the Can-Do's <u>and</u> the Science Skills as well.

Joanne says ....

"I really like science ! I try to get the Can-Do's right and I do my best in practical lessons. I worry a bit about the tests though "

- Don't worry Joanne ! Your teacher will help you to choose the correct level test for you. As you're such a keen scientist, you should be able to do well in them anyway.

Cathy says ....

"I'm not sure what I'm supposed to do in practicals. I'm a bit shy. How can I do well in 'Communication' ?"

- Be positive ! Look at the communication processes. To gain Foundation level, you must speak to your teacher, but it doesn't have to be in front of the whole class (and a whisper counts). Anyway, as your teacher gets to know you better he or she will help you.

8

What happens to all these Marks ?

The results of the three types of test will be recorded both by you and your teacher. In this way you will build up a record of your achievement in Science. Your teachers will periodically review this with you and suggest ways by which you may be able to improve your performance.

Reports will be written at the end of the year based on this record of achievement. They will be much more detailed than previous reports.

Finally, all the marks you gain in years 3, 4 and 5 will count towards your GCSE grade in Science. The third year is the foundation year to the course and the marks will only make up about one sixth of your overall GCSE grade, since it is recognised that you will improve throughout the course.

Your Record of Achievement.

Can-Do Tests

9

1.		Can use a microscope.
2.		Can make a slide.
5.		Can inoculate an agar plate.
6.		Can detect starch in food.
8.		Can use a balance.
9.		Can prepare a cutting of a plant.
10.		Can use a thermometer.
12.		Can filter a mixture.
13.		Can collect a sample of gas.
14.		Can test for & identify a gas.
16.		Can heat a substance safely.
19.		Can select a logic gate to solve a problem.
21.		Can connect a probe/sensor to a gate.
22.		Can measure accurately on any linear instrument.
23.		Can measure pulse rate.
24.		Can choose and use a Newton meter to measure force.
25.		Can identify both load and effort for any machine.

Your teacher will initial here when you can-do the test.

10   Science Skills

| | Level of Attainment | | | | | |
	Biol		Chem		Phys	
Observing						
Planning and Designing						
Communicating – Spoken						
Communicating – Non-spoken.						
Exploring and Investigating – Practically						
Exploring and Investigating – Data Search						
Collaborating effectively						
Concern for the Application of Scientific Knowledge within the Community						

F = Foundation, M = Merit, S = Special.

Your teacher will initial here to confirm the level reached.

Unit Tests	Date	Level		Date	Retest	
BIOLOGY						
Cells and Life						
Microbes						
Food and Digestion						
Reproductive Strategies						
CHEMISTRY						
Extracting materials						
Gases						
Materials						
Elements						
PHYSICS						
Energy						
Particles						
Biophysics and Sports Science						
Microelectronics						
Forces						

Your teacher will initial here, to confirm the level.

12 Homework Assignments

BIOLOGY

Cells and Life										
Microbes										
Food and Digestion										
Reproductive Strategies										

CHEMISTRY

Extracting materials										
Gases										
Materials										
Elements										

PHYSICS.

Energy										
Particles										
Biophysics and Sports Science										
Microelectronics										
Forces										

L = late   N = not completed

Discussions with your teacher.

At least once a term you will discuss your progress with your teacher. Helpful comments will be recorded here.

Comment	Date	Initials	
		yours	T.I.

14 Other Details

Record here other details which you think are relevant to your science education.

Your Science Skills Check List

OBSERVING.

15

You can gain FOUNDATION level if you are able to take at least ONE of the following :-

You can tick the ones you are able to do in Biology, Chemistry & Physics.

	Biol	Chem	Phys
F1. I can take a temperature, measure a length or take a meter reading accurately.			
F2. I can draw or describe the important details of an object			
F3. I can use a simple key to identify an object.			
F4. I can see and report an important change in an experiment			
You can gain MERIT level if you have reached foundation level and can also do at least one of the following :-			
M6. I can see if there is a pattern in the results of an experiment.			
M7. I can notice if any of my results don't fit in with the others.			
M8. I use a number of my senses when making observations.			
M9. I can draw or describe objects accurately.			
You can gain SPECIAL level if you have reached both foundation and merit levels and can also do at least ONE of the following :-			
S11. I make particularly accurate observations.			
S12 When I see an unexpected result I repeat the experiment to check it.			
S13 I can see and report in detail on the important changes that occur throughout an experiment.			

16

PLANNING AND DESIGNING

You can gain FOUNDATION level if you are
able to take at least ONE of the following :-

	Biol	Chem	Phys
F1. I can write about (or tell my teacher) how things need to be done to solve a simple problem.			
F2. I can devise an outline plan to solve a simple problem safely.			
F3. I can devise a plan which has a "fair test" in it, that is 'I only change one thing at a time'.			
You can gain MERIT level if you have reached foundation level and can also do at least one of the following :-			
M6. My plan has things in the right order and could be successful.			
M7. I have checked my plan by comparing it with others.			
M8. I can say how my plan has considered things like safety or accuracy.			
M9 I have listed observations and measurements that need to be taken.			
M10 My plan has made sure that all variables are controlled correctly.			
You can gain SPECIAL level if you have reached both foundation and merit levels and can also do at least ONE of the following :-			
S11 I have alternatives in case the main plan doesn't work.			
S12 My plan allows me to repeat readings so that my results are more reliable.			
S13 I have said if a 'control' is necessary.			
S14 My ordered plan will solve a complicated problem.			

COMMUNICATING - SPOKEN. **17**			
You can gain FOUNDATION level if you are able to take at least ONE of the following :-	Biol	Chem	Phys
F1 I listen to instructions and act on them.			
F2 I can ask questions or make sensible suggestions.			
F3 I can (with help if necessary) give a simple summary using some scientific words.			
You can gain MERIT level if you have reached foundation level and can also do at least one of the following :-			
M6 I can play a useful part in class discussion by listening and talking.			
M7 I can use the correct scientific words to describe apparatus or experiments.			
M8 I can talk clearly about an experiment and answer questions about it.			
M9 I am able to ask sensible questions which help me understand others.			
You can gain SPECIAL level if you have reached both foundation and merit levels and can also do at least ONE of the following :-			
S11 My arguments or explanations use scientific theory and/or experimental results.			
S12 I can explain scientific ideas in everyday language.			
S13 I can talk clearly about a science topic that I have prepared previously.			
S14 I am willing to contribute to scientific discussions.			

18 COMMUNICATING - NON-SPOKEN.

You can gain FOUNDATION level if you are
able to take at least ONE of the following :-

	Biol	Chem	Phys
F1 I can describe, in words (or by drawing a diagram or flowchart), the main features of something I can see.			
F2 I can record results accurately in the way my teacher asks me to.			
F3 I can draw and label diagrams.			
F4 I can show someone else how to do an experiment.			
F5 I can show that I have read and understood some scientific text.			
You can gain MERIT level if you have reached foundation level and can also do at least one of the following :-			
M6 I can produce ordered and accurate descriptions, diagrams and flowcharts.			
M7 I can decide how best to record my results in the standard scientific way.			
M8 I can change information from one form to another e.g. plot a graph from a table of values.			
M9 I choose to present information in an imaginative and interesting way.			
You can gain SPECIAL level if you have reached both foundation and merit levels and can also do at least ONE of the following :-			
S11 I use the correct scientific descriptions and symbols readily.			
S12 I can use theory and experimental results to produce a clear argument or explanation.			
S13 I use a wide range of techniques clearly and accurately when presenting information.			

Appendix 3

**TECHNICAL & VOCATIONAL
EDUCATION INITIATIVE**

FORM A   NAME

RECORD OF ACHIEVEMENT

PRE INTERVIEW QUESTIONNAIRE

Please complete this Form as neatly as possible and take it with you
when you go for your interview with your tutor. The information and
your first interview will be part of your contribution to your Record
of Achievement.

NAME :_____   FORM _____

OTHER NAMES : _____   TUTOR _____

AGE : _____   D.O.B. _____

DATE OF ENTRY TO SCHOOL : _____

OTHER SECONDARY SCHOOLS ATTENDED :

_____

_____

NAMES/AGES   _____
OF BROTHERS/SISTERS
        _____

NAME OF PARENT/GUARDIAN   _____

FULL POSTAL ADDRESS   _____

        _____

        _____

TELEPHONE NUMBER   _____

RECORDS OF ACHIEVEMENT

List the subjects/options/modules you are taking for your 4th/5th year. Try and use the correct subject title. Also include how many periods you spend on each subject.

SUBJECT	PERIODS
	TOTAL

Have you thought about a career/course you might take when you leave school? Give some details: _____

_____

_____

Which subject above will help you the most to achieve your career/course? _____

_____

_____

Are you happy with your option choice?   Yes/No
If no give details _____

_____

_____

What subject did you do well in your third year?_____

_____

_____

What do you hope to do well in during your fourth year?_____

_____

_____

List some interests/activities you do in school:_____

_____

_____

List some interests/activites you do out of school:_____

_____

_____

Describe an achievement you are particularly proud of:_____

_____

_____

RECORDS OF ACHIEVEMENT

Have you taken part in any school trips for work or pleasure.
Give details of:

_____

_____

_____

_____

Have you received any school awards during the past three years.
Attendance/form/sport/topic/academic.
Give details of:

_____

_____

_____

Do you make use of any local facilities? If so give details. (Leisure

Centres/cinema/clubs)

_____

_____

_____

Have you done/completed anything else in recent years that you would

like recording? Give details of:

On the scales below, which statement was true about you in
your third year.

	EXCELLENT	VERY GOOD	GOOD	AVERAGE	POOR
ATTENDANCE					
PUNCTUALITY					

	PERFECT	VERY TIDY	TIDY	UNTIDY	NOT IN SCHOOL DRESS
SCHOOL DRESS					

On the scale below what has your attendance/punctuality/school dress
been like since commencing the fourth year.

	EXCELLENT	VERY GOOD	GOOD	AVERAGE	POOR
ATTENDANCE					
PUNCTUALITY					
DRESS					

During your first interview with your Tutor is there anything you
would like to discuss?

Signed ....

Date ....

Appendix 4

I

NAME:.............................   FORM/SET:............

QUESTIONNAIRE IMPRESSIONS

TUTOR REVIEWS
4th:

5th:

CURRICULUM ROUTE

WORK EXPERIENCE

RESIDENTIALS

TESTIMONIAL
COMPLETED

OTHERS

PUNCTUALITY: 4th YEAR

PUNCTUALITY: 5th YEAR

ATTENDANCE: 4th YEAR

ATTENDANCE: 5th YEAR

AS A FRACTION

MAJOR ACHIEVEMENTS IN 3rd YEAR

2

CAREER THOUGHTS-

4th year

5th year

ACHIEVEMENTS AND INTERESTS

IN SCHOOL: 4th YEAR

IN SCHOOL: 5th YEAR

OUT OF SCHOOL: 4th YEAR

OUT OF SCHOOL: 5th YEAR

STUDENT ENQUIRIES

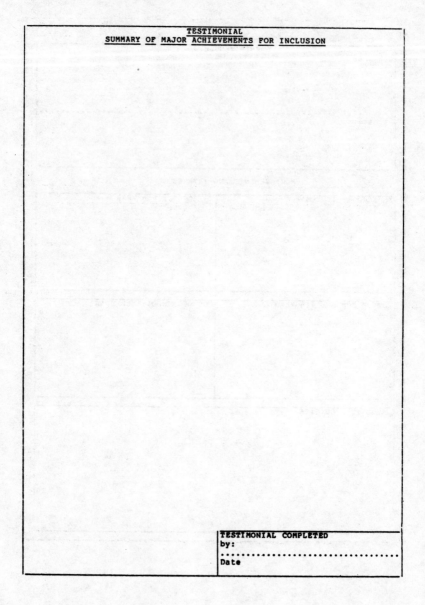

TESTIMONIAL
SUMMARY OF MAJOR ACHIEVEMENTS FOR INCLUSION

TESTIMONIAL COMPLETED
by:
....
Date

3

TARGETS SET:-
4th year

....

5th year

ADDITIONAL INFORMATION INSERTED BY STUDENT/STAFF

Appendix 5

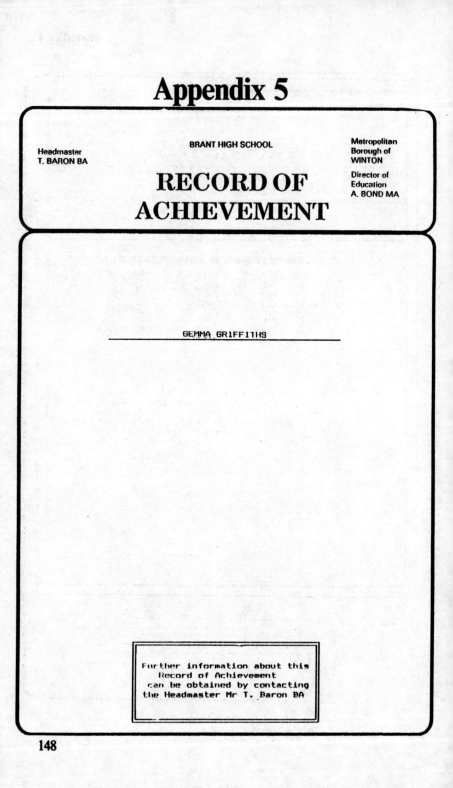

BRANT HIGH SCHOOL

Headmaster
T. BARON BA

Metropolitan
Borough of
WINTON

Director of
Education
A. BOND MA

RECORD OF ACHIEVEMENT

GEMMA GRIFFITHS

Further information about this
Record of Achievement
can be obtained by contacting
the Headmaster Mr T. Baron BA

BRANT HIGH SCHOOL

Metropolitan
Borough of
WINTON

Headmaster
T. BARON BA

RECORD OF
ACHIEVEMENT

Director of
Education
A. BOND MA

NORTHERN PARTNERSHIP FOR RECORDS OF ACHIEVEMENT

NPRA

This Record of Achievement has been developed
by Brant High School with the support of
Winton LEA as part of the NPRA Pilot Study
in the accreditation of centres. The school
has participated fully in the Pilot Study, has
been closely monitored by the LEA and the NPRA,
and has adopted approaches consistent with NPRA
guidelines.

March 1988

NPRA is a consortium of 37 Northern Local Education Authorities
and the five Boards of the Northern Examining Association

BRANT HIGH SCHOOL

Headmaster
T. BARON BA

Metropolitan
Borough of
WINTON

Director of
Education
A. BOND MA

TESTIMONIAL

Name GEMMA Griffiths

Attendance 137/191
Punctuality Excellent

Gemma has been a pupil at Brant High School for five years, and during this time she has participated in many extra-curricular activities. Gemma has been a member of the school netball and hockey teams and has represented her form on sports day at high jump. In the past year, Gemma has extended her leisure interests to include canoeing, rock climbing, roller skating and ice skating.

Gemma is following an integrated course of study which consists of several NEA Units and City and Guilds certificates in numeracy and communications. Gemma has successfully completed many of her NEA units and has received good reports from her subject teachers, who are pleased with her conscientiousness and the high standard of her work.

Gemma has completed a very successful work experience in the laundry at Whiston Hospital. She impressed her superviser with her mature attitude to work, and with her pleasant personality. Gemma enjoyed her placement and maintained a good working relationship with all the staff with whom she came into contact.

During my three years as Gemma's form tutor I have found her to be a pleasant, polite and well-mannered pupil who has a positive attitude towards school. Gemma is a well-behaved and articulate pupil who is popular within her peer group.

B.PYLE
Form Tutor

BRANT HIGH SCHOOL

Headmaster
T. BARON BA

Metropolitan
Borough of
WINTON

Director of
Education
A. BOND MA

CURRICULUM
PROFILE

Subject Area	Periods	Examination Entry
Information Technology	12	NEA
FSE	12	NEA City & Guilds Numeracy & Communication
Environmental Studies	4	NEA
Biology	4	NEA
PE/Games	4	
Modules	4	NEA

Total 40 Periods

BRANT HIGH SCHOOL

Headmaster
T. BARON BA

Metropolitan
Borough of
WINTON

Director of
Education
A. BOND MA

SUBJECT PROFILES

COMMUNICATION SKILLS

Gemma can read and understand written material and can look up information using an index and can find straightforward facts. She listens carefully and understands straightforward spoken information. She usually speaks clearly and is able to use a wide vocabulary.

Gemma speaks readily in class and her spelling and punctuation are usually correct in written work. She uses a wide vocabulary in written work and, when interested, can write with imagination.

NUMERACY

Gemma understands some mathematical concepts such as would be involved in number work, decimals and fractions. For this she has adequate recall. She is usually proficient in simple calculations and is able to set out the necessary steps in logical order. With guidance she is able to find correct solutions to problems. Gemma has also successfully completed two NEA Units in: The use of a Calculator and Everyday Budgeting.

J.BURKE

ENVIRONMENTAL STUDIES

Gemma understands some geographical concepts and has good recall. She always tries to present her work neatly and sets it out extremely well. With guidance, Gemma is able to analyse problems and find a solution. She has produced some very good work this year.

A.BAKER

TECHNOLOGY

Gemma can communicate design ideas graphically to a reasonable standard and is able, with moderate guidance, to solve some problems requiring creative thought. She produces an acceptable standard of practical work showing a reasonable amount of planning and displays some understanding of the subject but needs guidance. Gemma always shows interest and is well behaved.

B.DODD

BRANT HIGH SCHOOL

Headmaster
T. BARON BA

SUBJECT PROFILES

Metropolitan
Borough of
WINTON

Director of
Education
A. BOND MA

BIOLOGY

Gemma handles apparatus and materials correctly and can follow complicated instructions. She is usually able to make accurate observations, records results effectively if given a simple format or guidelines and is able to interpret data to produce logical conclusions when given some assistance.

Gemma is a very hard-working pupil who has a good grasp of the Biology syllabus.

B.PYLE

PHYSICAL EDUCATION

Gemma is capable of learning new techniques to a good standard and she has attained a reasonable level of ability in some activities. She occasionally displays creative awareness and she is a reasonably enthusiastic participant in some physical activities. Gemma usually co-operates with adults and pupils and she often takes the initiative as a spokesperson. She is reliable and has regard for safety.

B.FITTER

Headmaster
T. BARON BA

BRANT HIGH SCHOOL

Metropolitan
Borough of
WINTON

Director of
Education
A. BOND MA

CERTIFICATION
VERIFICATION

Metropolitan
Borough of
WINTON

Director of
Education
A. BOND MA

Statement of ACHIEVEMENT

Scheme of Unit Accreditation

This unit of work was validated by the Northern Examining Association. The title of this unit will appear on a final letter of credit to be issued to each student by the NEA.

Gemma Griffiths	25.12.71	Brant High
(Name)	(Date of Birth)	(School)

successfully completed the following unit of work.

WRITING A SHORT STORY

The student has demonstrated the ability to:-

1) choose a list of suitable words to be used in the story

2) set out the story with a suitable title, introductory paragraph and progression to a conclusion

3) read the story to other students in the group

4) evaluate their own and other students' stories

A. Bond

A. BOND
Borough Education Officer

Statement of ACHIEVEMENT

Metropolitan
Borough of
WINTON

Director of
Education
A. BOND MA

Scheme of Unit Accreditation

This unit of work was validated by the Northern Examining Association.
The title of this unit will appear on a final letter of credit to be issued to each
student by the NEA.

Gemma Griffiths	25.12.71	Brant High
(Name)	(Date of Birth)	(School)

successfully completed the following unit of work.

PLANNING A RESIDENTIAL EXPERIENCE

The student has demonstrated the ability to :-

1. Plan a balanced menu within a fixed budget and the limitations of the facilities

2. Draw up an equipment list for the activities to be undertaken

3. Decide the group compositions for duties and tasks e.g. accommodation, meals

4. Budget for the residential experience

The pupil has shown a knowledge of :-

5. Requirements for a balanced diet

A. Bond.

A. BOND
Borough Education Officer

156

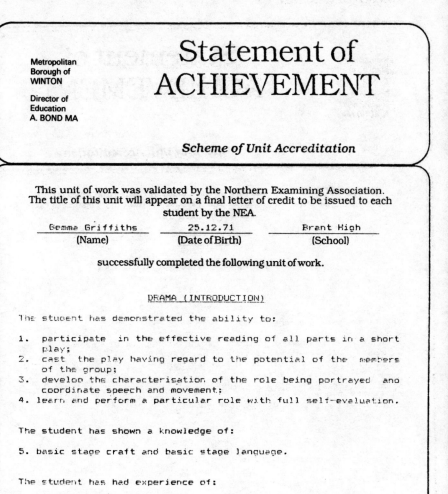

Statement of ACHIEVEMENT

Metropolitan
Borough of
WINTON

Director of
Education
A. BOND MA

Scheme of Unit Accreditation

This unit of work was validated by the Northern Examining Association. The title of this unit will appear on a final letter of credit to be issued to each student by the NEA.

Gemma Griffiths	25.12.71	Brant High
(Name)	(Date of Birth)	(School)

successfully completed the following unit of work.

DRAMA (INTRODUCTION)

The student has demonstrated the ability to:

1. participate in the effective reading of all parts in a short play;
2. cast the play having regard to the potential of the members of the group;
3. develop the characterisation of the role being portrayed and coordinate speech and movement;
4. learn and perform a particular role with full self-evaluation.

The student has shown a knowledge of:

5. basic stage craft and basic stage language.

The student has had experience of:

6. being involved in a performance on stage before an audience.

A. Bond

A. BOND
Borough Education Officer

157

Metropolitan
Borough of
WINTON

Director of
Education
A. BOND MA

Statement of
ACHIEVEMENT

Scheme of Unit Accreditation

This unit of work was validated by the Northern Examining Association.
The title of this unit will appear on a final letter of credit to be issued to each
student by the NEA.

Gemma Griffiths	25.12.71	. Brant High
(Name)	(Date of Birth)	(School)

successfully completed the following unit of work.

COMMUNITY SERVICE

The student has demonstrated the ability to:

1. arrive at placement punctually and appropriately dressed;
2. assist placement staff in any way asked;
3. observe client activity and behaviour;
4. survey client interests;
5. interview at least one client;
6. assess own achievement;
7. maintain a record of the placements.

A. Bond .

A. BOND
Borough Education Officer

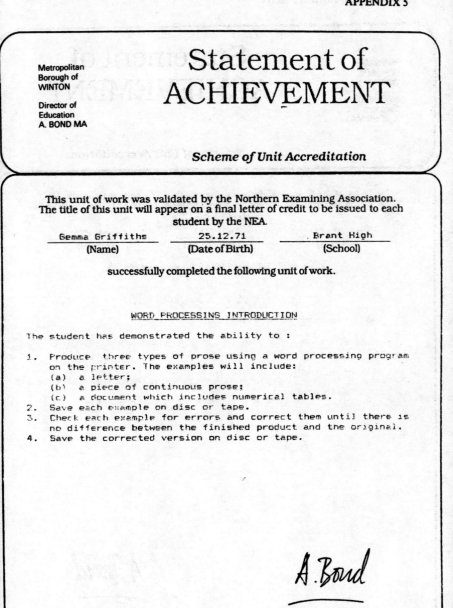

Metropolitan
Borough of
WINTON

Director of
Education
A. BOND MA

Statement of
ACHIEVEMENT

Scheme of Unit Accreditation

This unit of work was validated by the Northern Examining Association.
The title of this unit will appear on a final letter of credit to be issued to each
student by the NEA.

Gemma Griffiths	25.12.71	Brant High
(Name)	(Date of Birth)	(School)

successfully completed the following unit of work.

WORD PROCESSING INTRODUCTION

The student has demonstrated the ability to :

1. Produce three types of prose using a word processing program
   on the printer. The examples will include:
   (a) a letter;
   (b) a piece of continuous prose;
   (c) a document which includes numerical tables.
2. Save each example on disc or tape.
3. Check each example for errors and correct them until there is
   no difference between the finished product and the original.
4. Save the corrected version on disc or tape.

A. Bond

A. BOND
Borough Education Officer

Statement of ACHIEVEMENT

Metropolitan
Borough of
WINTON

Director of
Education
A. BOND MA

Scheme of Unit Accreditation

This unit of work was validated by the Northern Examining Association. The title of this unit will appear on a final letter of credit to be issued to each student by the NEA.

Gemma Griffiths	25.12.71	Brant High
(Name)	(Date of Birth)	(School)

successfully completed the following unit of work.

HEALTH STUDIES - REPRODUCTION

The pupil has demonstrated the ability to:

1. explain the difference between asexual and sexual reproduction;
2. describe the human reproductive system and some of the diseases which may result from sexual activities;
3. describe the development of the foetus and the needs for pre-birth care;
4. describe the nature and purpose of helping agencies;

A. Bond .

A. BOND
Borough Education Officer